HIKING
GRAND TETON
NATIONAL PARK

Help Us Keep This Guide Up to Date

Every effort has been made by the author and editors to make this guide as accurate and use-ful as possible. However, many things can change after a guide is published—trails are rerouted, regulations change, facilities come under new management, and so forth.

We welcome your comments concerning your experiences with this guide and how you feel it could be improved and kept up to date. While we may not be able to respond to all com-ments and suggestions, we'll take them to heart, and we'll also make certain to share them with the author. Please send your comments and suggestions to the following address:

Globe Pequot Press
Reader Response/Editorial Department
246 Goose Lane
Guilford, CT 06437

Or you may e-mail us at:

editorial@falcon.com

Thanks for your input, and happy trails!

HIKING GRAND TETON NATIONAL PARK

A GUIDE TO THE PARK'S GREATEST HIKING ADVENTURES

FOURTH EDITION

Bill Schneider

FALCONGUIDES

GUILFORD, CONNECTICUT

FALCONGUIDES®

An imprint of The Rowman & Littlefield Publishing Group, Inc.
4501 Forbes Blvd., Suite 200
Lanham, MD 20706
www.rowman.com

Falcon and FalconGuides are registered trademarks and Make Adventure Your Story is a trademark of The Rowman & Littlefield Publishing Group, Inc.

Distributed by NATIONAL BOOK NETWORK

British Library Cataloguing in Publication Information available

Library of Congress Cataloging-in-Publication Data available

ISBN 978-1-4930-3003-3 (paperback)

ISBN 978-1-4930-3004-0 (e-book)

∞™ The paper used in this publication meets the minimum requirements of American National Standard for Information Sciences—Permanence of Paper for Printed Library Materials, ANSI/NISO Z39.48-1992.

Printed in the United States of America

WILDERNESS is . . .

The FREEDOM to experience true wildness . . . to hear only nature's music . . . to study the little secrets of the natural world . . . and to enjoy the quiet and solitude so rare in the stressful life we now live.

The CHALLENGE to learn and respect wild country . . . to be self-reliant . . . to take your time . . . to test your physical abilities . . . to courteously share the last blank spots on the map with others . . . and to fully enjoy your experience while leaving no trace of your passing.

The OPPORTUNITY to discover why wilderness is priceless . . . to see the threats to your wilderness . . . to decide to devote part of yourself to preserving more of it . . . and to encourage others to do the same.

—Bill Schneider

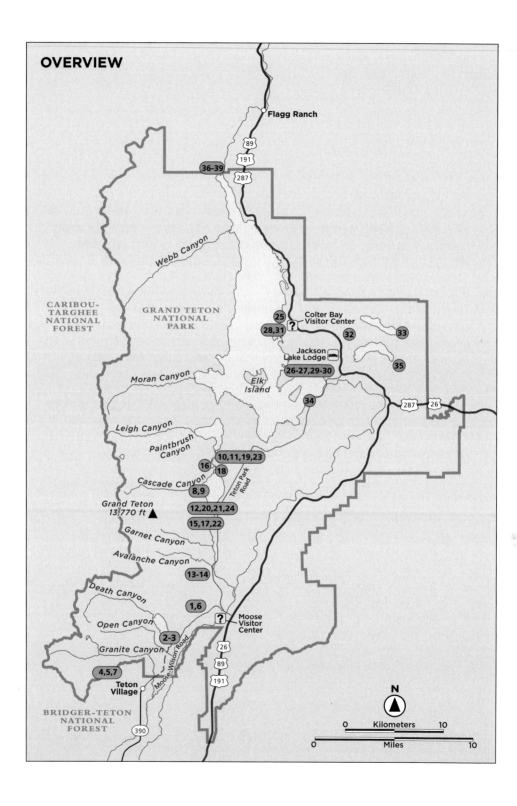

OVERVIEW

Flagg Ranch

89
191

36-39

287

Webb Canyon

CARIBOU-
TARGHEE
NATIONAL
FOREST

GRAND TETON
NATIONAL
PARK

25
28,31
?

Colter Bay
Visitor Center

32

33

Jackson
Lake Lodge

Moran Canyon

Elk
Island

26-27,29-30

35

Leigh Canyon

34

287

26

Paintbrush
Canyon

10,11,19,23

16
18

Cascade Canyon

8,9

Teton Park Road

Grand Teton
13,770 ft ▲

12,20,21,24

15,17,22

Garnet Canyon

Avalanche Canyon

13-14

Death Canyon

1,6

Open Canyon

?

Moose
Visitor
Center

2-3

26

Granite Canyon

Moose-Wilson Road

89

4,5,7

191

Teton
Village

BRIDGER-TETON
NATIONAL
FOREST

390

N
▲

0   Kilometers   10

0   Miles   10

CONTENTS

THE HIKES

Teton Village Area

Jenny Lake Area

PREFACE: HIKING AMERICA'S MOST FAMOUS WILDERNESS SKYLINE

Grand Teton National Park probably has the most famous natural skyline in the country. This prominent horizon shows up every year on millions of postcards, calendars, magazine and book covers, and television ads. But just looking at it is not enough. You need to go there and hike through the deep canyons gouged out by glaciers and over the big divides to feel the true essence of these mountains.

For outstanding mountain scenery, Grand Teton ranks, quite simply, as the best. You would have to really try hard not to have a memorable hike. As you plan your trip, here are a few things you might want to know about hiking in Grand Teton National Park.

Prime season: The best time to hike Grand Teton is August and September. Snow buries the high peaks each winter and grips the high trails such as Hurricane Pass, Paintbrush Divide, and Moose Basin Divide until at least mid-July, sometimes into August.

Weather: It can snow any day of the year in Grand Teton, so always be prepared for it. The normal summer weather pattern (if there is such a thing) is clear mornings with thundershowers in the mid-afternoon, followed by clear, cool evenings. This means early-morning hikers usually enjoy better weather, and they more often get their tents set up before it rains. June can frequently (but not always) be a fairly wet month in Grand Teton.

Sharing: Hikers don't have the trails of Grand Teton to themselves. They share those trails not only with a growing number of hikers and climbers but also with backcountry horse riders. If you meet a stock party on the trail, yield by moving off the trail on the downhill side and quietly let the stock animals pass.

Moose country: This is definitely moose country. In fact, it's difficult to go hiking all day in Grand Teton without seeing a moose. Enjoy watching them, but stay out of the way. Moose do not yield to hikers.

Bears: Grand Teton has bears, both the black bear and its larger, more cantankerous cousin, the grizzly. Black bears have always been common throughout the park, and now, grizzlies are often seen, not only in the northern and less frequently used sections of the park, but also in the more heavily used southern sections. All bears—black and grizzly— are dangerous, so take all the standard precautions.

The canyons: Many hikes, such as Holly Lake, Cascade Canyon, Paintbrush Divide and others, leave the valley floor and penetrate the Teton Range via deep, glacier-scoured canyons. The canyons serve as pathways into the high peaks. They're usually steep in the first few miles, then they level out, and suddenly, you're surrounded by steep-walled majesty on your way up a spectacular pass or divide.

Finding solitude: Grand Teton is so heavily used by hikers and climbers that on some trails, they seem to be everywhere. You can find solitude, however, especially in the

North Trails area, as well as in a few other areas, but probably not at Lake Solitude, a very popular hiking destination. If you want to be lonely for a change, check through the hike descriptions until you find a lightly used route.

Bugs: Perhaps the two seasons I hiked Grand Teton were off years for the mosquito, but it sure seems like the park has fewer mosquitoes than most places in the Rocky Mountains. In Montana's Beartooths or in Yellowstone, the mosquitoes can block out the sun on a clear day, but in Grand Teton, I took out the repellent only once (in Glade Creek), which is unusual to say the least.

Large furry things on the road: When hurrying to get to the trailhead in the early-morning hours or when feeling impatient while driving home in the evening, be especially watchful for large wildlife on the roadways. Hitting a moose or bison will certainly ruin your day, and it's even harder on the animal.

Hiker friendly: In some national parks it's easy to feel overregulated. However, Grand Teton National Park has made special efforts to provide freedom of choice and to limit the number of regulations.

Research pays: Plan your trip (and alternatives to it) before you head for Grand Teton. This saves valuable time—and you want to spend that time hiking instead of driving around or waiting in traffic jams, right? You may not be able to get the permit you want, and bear management, forest fires, high water, road construction, and other factors can change things. So, have a backup plan.

You can find more details on these topics in the following pages.

Snake River Overlook, featuring America's wilderness skyline CASEY SCHNEIDER

MEET YOUR GUIDE

Bill Schneider has spent a half-century hiking trails all across America. It all started in college in the late-1960s when he landed a job that paid him to hike, working on the trail crew in Glacier National Park. He spent the 1970s publishing *Montana Outdoors* magazine for the Montana Department of Fish, Wildlife & Parks and covering as many miles of trails as possible on weekends and holidays.

In 1979 Bill and his partner, Mike Sample, founded Falcon Publishing, gradually building it for the next 20 years. Along the way, Bill wrote twenty-one books and hundreds of magazine articles on wildlife, outdoor recreation, and conservation issues.

For 12 years, he taught classes on bicycling, backpacking, zero-impact camping, and hiking in bear country for the Yellowstone Institute, a nonprofit educational organization in Yellowstone National Park.

In 2000 Bill retired from his position as president of Falcon Publishing (now part of Rowman & Littlefield) after it had grown into the premier publisher of outdoor recreation guidebooks with more than 800 titles in print. He stayed in the publishing game for six more years working as a consultant and acquisition editor for the Lyons Press and Falcon imprints and as Travel and Outdoor editor for NewWest.Net, a regional online magazine, where he wrote a weekly *Wild Bill* column devoted to what he called "outdoor politics."

He now lives in Helena, Montana, with his wife, Marnie, works as little as possible, and spends almost every day hiking, bicycling, or fishing.

FIVE HIKING TIPS FROM BILL

1. Tell somebody where you're hiking and when you expect to return. **2.** Take plenty of water and drink frequently throughout the hike. **3.** Be bear aware and always carry bear spray, anywhere in Grand Teton National Park. Know how to use it and keep it instantly accessible. **4.** Buy a separate map instead of depending on the small maps in this book. **5.** Hike early, starting at dawn ideally, to avoid midday heat and the crowds common on many park trails.

Books in Print by Bill Schneider

Backpacking Tips (coauthor)

Backpacker Magazine's Bear Country Behavior

Bear Aware: A Quick Reference Bear Country Survival Guide

Best Backpacking Vacations Northern Rockies

Best Easy Day Hikes Absaroka-Beartooth Wilderness

Best Easy Day Hikes Canyonlands and Arches

Best Easy Day Hikes Grand Teton

Best Easy Day Hikes Yellowstone

Best Hikes on the Continental Divide (coauthor)

Hiking Canyonlands and Arches National Parks

Hiking Carlsbad Caverns and Guadalupe Mountains National Parks

Hiking Grand Teton National Park

Hiking Montana (coauthor)

Hiking Montana: Bozeman

Hiking the Absaroka-Beartooth Wilderness

Hiking Yellowstone National Park

The Tree Giants

Where the Grizzly Walks

The Moose-Wilson Road runs north of Teton Village into the park.
NATIONAL PARK SERVICE

USING THIS GUIDEBOOK

To help you choose a hike, we preface each entry with some basic information, including type of hike, difficulty ratings, and distance covered. Our basic maps and elevation profiles supplement this information with quick visuals. To use these tools effectively, please note the explanations below.

TYPES OF HIKES

Hikes have been organized into the following categories:

Loop: Starts and finishes at the same trailhead, with no (or very little) retracing of your steps. Sometimes the definition of loop is stretched to include "lollipops" where you retrace the first part of the route and trips that involve a short walk on a road at the end of the hike to get back to your vehicle.

Shuttle: A point-to-point trip that requires two vehicles (one left at each end of the trail) or a prearranged pickup at a designated time and place. One good way to manage the logistical problems of shuttles is to arrange for another party to start at the other end of the trail. The two parties meet at a predetermined point and then trade keys. When finished, they drive each other's vehicles home.

Out and back: Traveling to a specific destination, then retracing your steps back to the trailhead.

Base camp: Any hike on which you spend several nights at the same campsite, using the extra days for fishing, climbing, relaxing, or day hiking.

HIKE RATINGS

To help plan your trip, I've rated hikes by difficulty. However, ratings serve only as general guides, not the final word. What is difficult to one hiker may be easy to another. Difficulty ratings take into account both how long and how strenuous a route is. Following are general definitions of the ratings.

Easy: Suitable for any hiker, including children or elderly people, without serious elevation gain, hazardous sections, or places where the trail is faint.

Moderate: Suitable for hikers who have some experience and at least an average fitness level. Probably not suitable for children or the elderly unless they have an above-average level of fitness. The hike may have some short sections where the trail is difficult to follow, and it often includes some hills.

Difficult: Suitable for experienced hikers with above-average fitness level, often with sections of the trail that are difficult to follow or even some off-trail sections that could require knowledge of route-finding with a topo map and compass, sometimes with serious elevation gain and possibly some hazardous conditions.

CAMPSITE RATINGS

In several instances, I refer to campsites as "five-star," "four-star," "three-star," etc. This generally describes my nonscientific evaluation of the campsite but does not relate to any statistical standard. "Five-star" campgrounds, like top hotels and restaurants, are the best, in my opinion.

DISTANCES

Most distances come from NPS signs and brochures, but I've had to estimate some trail mileage. Since it's so difficult and time-consuming to precisely measure trails, most distances listed in any guidebook, on trail signs, and in park brochures are usually estimates. In Grand Teton you may find minor inconsistencies between signs, brochures, and this book, but these are rarely significant.

Keep in mind that distance is often less important than difficulty. A 2-mile, rocky, uphill trail can take longer and require more effort than 4 miles on a well-contoured trail on flat terrain. The punch line is, don't get excited if the distance is slightly off.

MAPS

The maps in this guidebook serve as general guides only. They lack adequate detail and don't cover enough territory to be used on their own in the field. You definitely should take a better map on any hike.

ELEVATION PROFILES

This book uses elevation profiles to provide an idea of the elevation gain and loss you will encounter along each hike. The vertical axis of the profiles shows the distance climbed in feet. Because of variations in scale, some elevation profiles may appear to show gradual hills as steep or steep hills as gradual, so be sure to check the Distance in the hike specs as well as the vertical axis to see the scale of elevation changes. Hikes with little or no elevation gain do not have elevation profiles.

NOTES ON MAPS

Topographic maps are essential companions to the activities in this guide. Falcon has partnered with National Geographic to provide the best mapping resources. Each activity is accompanied by a detailed map and the name of the National Geographic TOPO! map (USGS), which can be downloaded for free from natgeomaps.com.

If the activity takes place on a National Geographic Trails Illustrated map, it will be noted. Continually setting the standard for accuracy, each Trails Illustrated topographic map is crafted in conjunction with local land managers and undergoes rigorous review and enhancement before being printed on waterproof, tear-resistant material. Trails Illustrated maps and information about their digital versions, which can be used on mobile GPS applications, can be found at natgeomaps.com.

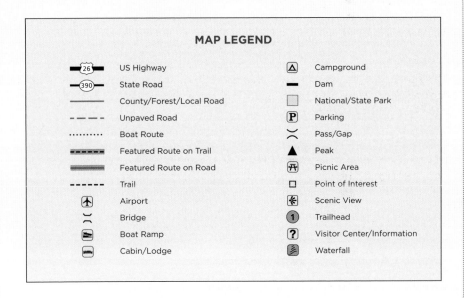

MAP LEGEND

26	US Highway	Campground
390	State Road	Dam
	County/Forest/Local Road	National/State Park
	Unpaved Road	Parking
	Boat Route	Pass/Gap
	Featured Route on Trail	Peak
	Featured Route on Road	Picnic Area
	Trail	Point of Interest
	Airport	Scenic View
	Bridge	Trailhead
	Boat Ramp	Visitor Center/Information
	Cabin/Lodge	Waterfall

The scenery changes when hikers get above timberline along Cascade Creek.
CASEY SCHNEIDER

BEFORE YOU HIT THE TRAIL

It's amazing how pleasant and stress free your hiking vacation to Grand Teton National Park can be when it's well planned. The following information should help you plan your trip.

GETTING THERE

Grand Teton National Park is in northwestern Wyoming, just south of Yellowstone National Park. You can drive to the park from Salt Lake City on I-15 north to Logan, Utah, turning on US 89 through Idaho and Wyoming to Jackson, Wyoming, and Grand Teton National Park. You can also take US 26 east from Idaho Falls, Idaho, to Jackson or west from Dubois or Casper, Wyoming. From Montana, you can drive through Yellowstone National Park (slow but scenic) or take US 20 south of West Yellowstone, Montana, and turn off on ID 32/33 over Teton Pass to Jackson, Wyoming.

Since federal highways pass through the park, you can see parts of Grand Teton without paying an entrance fee. Entrance stations are located on Teton Park Road just west of the Moose Visitor Center, at Moran Junction, and on Moose-Wilson Road just south of the Granite Canyon Trailhead. Expect to pay a fee to enter the park at these stations.

The park roads are well maintained but only two lanes wide and often crowded with traffic, including bicycles and other slow-moving vehicles. If you drive during midday, don't be in a hurry.

You can also fly to a small airport with limited jet service just north of Jackson, Wyoming. The airport is actually within the boundaries of the park.

GETTING BACKCOUNTRY PERMITS

In Grand Teton National Park, you must have a permit to stay overnight in the backcountry. Get these permits at the visitor centers at Moose and Colter Bay and at the Jenny Lake Ranger Station. To make the permitting process go more smoothly, read the backcountry camping brochure, which you can find on the park's website, www.nps.gov/grte, or you can request a copy by writing or calling the park.

Backcountry Office
Grand Teton National Park
PO Drawer 170
Moose, WY 83012-0170
(307) 739-3309
(307) 739-3438 (fax)

Columbine
NATIONAL PARK SERVICE

The park has an excellent website that explains in detail the entire process for getting a backcountry camping permit. Things often change year to year, so no need to repeat the current details here. You have to go to the website anyway, this year and every future year this book is in print.

Grand Teton has a backcountry permit reservation system. Make your reservation between the first Wednesday in January and May 15. The advanced reservation costs $35 per trip or $25 for in-person walk-up permits obtained at the park's visitor centers or ranger stations, regardless of the number of people or length of the trip. The NPS allows up to one-third of the designated sites to be reserved. The rest go out on a first-come, first-served basis. Permits requested at park visitor centers and ranger stations must be obtained no more than 24 hours before the start of your trip.

You must make advanced reservations online. Go to the park's website and click on Backcountry Reservations for details.

In any case, you need the following information: name, address, daytime phone, number of people in your party, preferred campsites, and preferred dates. If possible, include alternate campsites and dates.

Phone reservations are not accepted, but you can get information by calling (307) 739-3309 or (307) 739-3397.

Your reservation holds your permit, but you still need to pick it up no later than 10 a.m. the day your trip starts. If you fail to pick it up by 10 a.m., it will become available to others. If you're running a little late, you can call ahead and the National Park Service (NPS) will hold your permit.

If you have a reservation but are unable to take the trip, be sure to notify the NPS and cancel your reservation so the campsites can be made available to others. The NPS does not issue refunds for cancellations.

BACKCOUNTRY CAMPING POLICY

Some national parks have policies that can hardly be described as "hiker friendly," and consequently it's easy to feel overregulated. However, Grand Teton has a hiker-friendly backcountry policy. For example, consider these long-range goals in the park's backcountry management plan:

- Provide visitors to the backcountry with a high-quality experience.
- Provide for a range of levels of solitude.
- Provide for visitor use of the backcountry with a minimum level of restrictions.
- Provide hikers in pristine areas with the opportunity to have the same type of wilderness experience that people would have had before Europeans arrived in this area.

Jenny Lake and Cascade Canyon
NATIONAL PARK SERVICE

To allow more people to enjoy the backcountry, the park limits use for each hiker to no more than 2 nights in the same campsite and to 10 nights per summer. Quotas are set to prevent overuse, and party size is limited to six people for most campsites. If you have a larger party (up to twelve allowed), you must camp at a designated group site.

In 1973 the NPS banned all campfires in the park above 7,000 feet elevation. Only designated, low-elevation sites have fire grills where campfires can be built.

Backcountry camping is allowed in camping zones and at designated sites at some backcountry lakes. Within some camping zones, there are "indicated" campsites. The sites are usually convenient and well placed. While visiting a camping zone, you aren't required to stay in an indicated campsite. You can set up a no-impact camp anywhere in a camping zone. In some cases, the NPS also allows off-trail camping outside of camping zones.

BACKCOUNTRY USE REGULATIONS

Backcountry use regulations aren't intended to complicate your life. They help preserve the natural landscape and protect park visitors. The following regulations are distributed to hikers when they get their permits.

In Grand Teton, you must do the following:

- Have a permit for all overnight stays in the backcountry.
- Carefully follow the instructions on the permit.
- Build campfires only in designated fire pits at certain low-elevation campsites below 7,000 feet.

- Use only collected dead and downed wood. Keep fires small, and do not leave them unattended. Backpacking stoves are encouraged.
- Store unattended food or garbage in metal food storage lockers located at many campsites and camping zones or in portable bear-resistant food containers, available for free loan at visitor centers and ranger stations with a valid backcountry permit.
- Carry out all trash. If you can pack it in, you can pack it out.
- Have a valid Wyoming state fishing permit if you're fishing the waters of Grand Teton.

In Grand Teton, don't:

- Feed, touch, tease, frighten, or intentionally disturb wildlife.
- Take pets into the backcountry.
- Make campsite "improvements" such as fire rings, rock walls, log benches, drainage, trenches.
- Possess or operate a motorized vehicle, bicycle, wheeled vehicle, or cart in any undeveloped area or on any backcountry trail.
- Dispose of human waste within 200 feet of any water source or campsite or within sight of a trail.
- Possess, destroy, injure, deface, remove, dig, or disturb from its natural state any plant, rock, animal, mineral, cultural, or archaeological resource.
- Use or possess weapons, traps, or nets.
- Cut switchbacks.
- Wash dishes or bathe in park streams or lakes.

Bison grazing in the shadow of the Teton Range
NATIONAL PARK SERVICE

FOR MORE INFORMATION

For a great summary of basic facts on visiting Grand Teton, call the main park number and ask for a copy of the *Grand Teton Guide*, a free newspaper published by the Grand Teton Association. You can also get a copy at the entrance stations. The paper contains a list of commercial services in and near the park, updates on park road construction, lists of ranger-led activities, events and guided tours, campgrounds, medical and emergency services and facilities, area museums, special exhibits, plus lots more useful information. The *Grand Teton Guide* will answer most of your questions about park services. Because of budget cuts, the NPS is sometimes unable to keep up with all visitor inquiries, so please be patient when trying to get your questions answered. There are many books and other publications about Grand Teton that offer a wealth of excellent information, and they often provide a better way to get information than calling the park. Many of these publications are available at park visitor centers.

Contact the park at this address and phone number:

National Park Service
Park Headquarters
PO Drawer 170
Moose, WY 83012-0170
(307) 739-3309
www.nps.gov/grte

EMERGENCY MEDICAL SERVICES

In case of an emergency, call 911. You can also call the park's main dispatch number (307-739-3300) to report an emergency. Because of its remote location, the park has limited medical facilities. You can find limited care facilities at the Grand Teton Medical Clinic at Jackson Lake Lodge and at St. John's Hospital in Jackson, Wyoming.

TRAIL FINDER

HIKES TO BACKCOUNTRY LAKES

1   Phelps Lake
2   LSR Preserve Small Loop
3   LSR Preserve Big Loop
4   Marion Lake
7   The Teton Crest
10 Leigh Lake
11 String Lake
13 Taggart Lake
14 Bradley Lake
16 Bearpaw and Trapper Lakes
17 Surprise and Amphitheater Lakes
18 Jenny Lake
19 Holly Lake
21 Lake Solitude
22 Valley Trail
23 Paintbrush Divide
24 The Grand Teton Loop
28 Swan Lake and Heron Pond
31 Hermitage Point
33 Two Ocean Lake
35 Emma Matilda Lake

HIKES ALONG STREAMS

2   LSR Preserve Small Loop
3   LSR Preserve Big Loop
5   Rendezvous Mountain and Granite Canyon
6   Death Canyon and the Mount Hunt Divide
15 Garnet Canyon
20 Cascade Canyon
21 Lake Solitude
23 Paintbrush Divide

36 Glade Creek
38 Jackass Pass
39 Moose Basin Divide

HIKES TO WATERFALLS

8   Hidden Falls
18 Jenny Lake
20 Cascade Canyon

HIKES THROUGH ALPINE COUNTRY

4   Marion Lake
5   Rendezvous Mountain and Granite Canyon
6   Death Canyon and the Mount Hunt Divide
7   The Teton Crest
17 Surprise and Amphitheater Lakes
21 Lake Solitude
23 Paintbrush Divide
24 The Grand Teton Loop
38 Jackass Pass
39 Moose Basin Divide

HIKES TO MOUNTAINTOPS

5   Rendezvous Mountain and Granite Canyon
32 Grand View Point
34 Signal Mountain

HIKES WITH LOTS OF WILDFLOWERS

4   Marion Lake
5   Rendezvous Mountain and Granite Canyon

7 The Teton Crest
19 Holly Lake
20 Cascade Canyon
21 Lake Solitude
23 Paintbrush Divide
30 Lookout Rock
39 Moose Basin Divide

GOOD HIKES FOR SEEING WILDLIFE

12 Moose Ponds
27 Christian Pond
28 Swan Lake and Heron Pond
31 Hermitage Point
33 Two Ocean Lake
36 Glade Creek
39 Moose Basin Divide

HIKES ON REALLY FLAT TRAILS

10 Leigh Lake
11 String Lake
16 Bearpaw and Trapper Lakes
18 Jenny Lake
25 Lakeshore Trail
28 Swan Lake and Heron Pond
29 Willow Flats
31 Hermitage Point

GREAT HIKES FOR SMALL CHILDREN

2 LSR Preserve Small Loop
10 Leigh Lake
25 Lakeshore Trail
26 Lunch Tree Hill
27 Christian Pond
28 Swan Lake and Heron Pond
29 Willow Flats

EASY OVERNIGHTERS

1 Phelps Lake
10 Leigh Lake

MODERATE OVERNIGHTERS

4 Marion Lake
16 Bearpaw and Trapper Lakes
19 Holly Lake
22 Valley Trail
31 Hermitage Point

DIFFICULT OVERNIGHTERS

21 Lake Solitude
37 Elk Ridge

LONG BACKPACKING TRIPS

5 Rendezvous Mountain and Granite Canyon
6 Death Canyon and the Mount Hunt Divide
7 The Teton Crest
23 Paintbrush Divide
24 The Grand Teton Loop
38 Jackass Pass
39 Moose Basin Divide

EARLY-SEASON HIKES

1 Phelps Lake
2 LSR Preserve Small Loop
10 Leigh Lake
11 String Lake
13 Taggart Lake
14 Bradley Lake
16 Bearpaw and Trapper Lakes
18 Jenny Lake
22 Valley Trail
25 Lakeshore Trail
27 Christian Pond
28 Swan Lake and Heron Pond
29 Willow Flats
31 Hermitage Point

ZERO IMPACT

Going into a national park such as Grand Teton is like visiting a famous museum. You obviously do not want to leave your mark on an art treasure in the museum. If everybody going through the museum leaves one little mark, the piece of art will be quickly destroyed—and of what value is a big building full of trashed art? The same goes for a pristine wilderness such as Grand Teton, which is as magnificent as any masterpiece by any artist. If we all leave just one little mark on the landscape, the wilderness will soon be despoiled.

A wilderness can accommodate human use as long as everybody behaves, but a few thoughtless or uninformed visitors can ruin it for everybody who follows. All wilderness users have a responsibility to know and follow the rules of no-trace camping.

Today most wilderness users want to walk softly, but some aren't aware that they have poor manners. Often their actions are dictated by the outdated habits of a previous generation of campers who cut green boughs for evening shelters, built campfires with fire rings, and dug trenches around tents. In the 1950s these "camping rules" may have been acceptable, but they leave long-lasting scars, and today such behavior is absolutely unacceptable. The wilderness is shrinking, and the number of users is mushrooming. More and more camping areas show unsightly signs of heavy use.

Consequently, a new code of ethics is growing out of the necessity of coping with the unending waves of people who want a perfect wilderness experience. Today we all must leave no clues that we have gone before. Canoeists can look behind the canoe and see no trace of their passing. Hikers, mountain bikers, and four-wheelers should have the same goal. Enjoy the wilderness, but leave no trace of your visit.

Three FalconGuide Principles of Zero Impact

- Leave with everything you brought.
- Leave no sign of your visit.
- Leave the landscape as you found it.

Most of us know better than to litter—in or out of the wilderness. Be sure you leave nothing, regardless of how small it is, along the trail or at the campsite. This means you should pack out everything, including orange peels, flip tops, cigarette butts, and gum wrappers. Also, pick up any trash that others leave behind.

Follow the main trail. Avoid cutting switchbacks and walking on vegetation beside the trail.

Don't pick up "souvenirs," such as rocks, antlers, or wildflowers. The next person wants to see them, too, and collecting such souvenirs violates park regulations.

Avoid making loud noises that may disturb others. Remember, sound travels easily across lakes and open areas. Be courteous.

Carry a lightweight trowel to bury human waste 6 to 8 inches deep, and pack out used toilet paper. Keep human waste at least 200 feet from any water source.

Finally, and perhaps most importantly, strictly follow the pack-in/pack-out rule. If you carry something into the backcountry, consume it or carry it out.

Have zero impact—and put your ear to the ground in the wilderness and listen carefully. Thousands of people coming behind you are thanking you for your courtesy and good sense.

MAKE IT A SAFE TRIP

The Scouts have been guided for decades by what is perhaps the best single piece of safety advice: "Be Prepared!" For starters, this means carrying survival and first-aid materials, proper clothing, compass, and topographic map—and knowing how to use them.

Perhaps the second-best piece of safety advice is to tell somebody where you're going and when you plan to return. Pilots must file flight plans before every trip, and anybody venturing into a blank spot on the map should do the same. File your "flight plan" with a friend or relative before taking off.

Close behind your flight plan and being prepared with proper equipment is physical conditioning. Being fit not only makes wilderness travel more fun, but it also makes it safer. To whet your appetite for more knowledge of wilderness safety and preparedness, following are a few more tips:

- Check the weather forecast. Be careful not to get caught at high altitude by a bad storm or along a stream in a flash flood. Watch cloud formations closely so you don't get stranded on a ridgeline during a lightning storm. Avoid traveling during prolonged periods of cold weather.

- Avoid traveling alone in the wilderness.

- Keep your party together.

- Study basic survival and first aid before leaving home.

- Don't eat wild plants unless you have positively identified them.

- Before you leave for the trailhead, find out as much as you can about the route, especially the potential hazards.

- Don't exhaust yourself or other members of your party by traveling too far or too fast. Let the slowest person set the pace.

- Don't wait until you're confused to look at your maps. Follow them as you go along, from the moment you start moving up the trail, so you have a continual fix on your location.

- If you get lost, don't panic. Sit down and relax for a few minutes while you carefully check your topo map and take a reading with your compass. Confidently plan your next move. It's often smart to retrace your steps until you find familiar ground, even if you think it might lengthen your trip. Lots of people get temporarily lost in the wilderness and survive—usually by calmly and rationally dealing with the situation.

- Stay clear of all wild animals.

- Take a first-aid kit that includes, at a minimum, the following items: sewing needle, snakebite kit, aspirin, antibacterial ointment, two antiseptic swabs, two butterfly bandages, adhesive tape, four adhesive strips, four gauze pads, two triangular bandages, codeine tablets, two inflatable splints, Moleskin or Second Skin for blisters, one roll of 3-inch gauze, a CPR shield, rubber gloves, and lightweight first-aid instructions.

- Take a survival kit that includes, at a minimum, the following items: compass, whistle, matches in a waterproof container, cigarette lighter, candle, signal mirror, flashlight, fire starter, aluminum foil, water purification tablets, space blanket, and flare.

- Last but not least, don't forget that the best defense against unexpected hazards is knowledge. Read up on the latest in wilderness safety information.

LIGHTNING: YOU MIGHT NEVER KNOW WHAT HIT YOU

The high-altitude topography of Grand Teton is prone to sudden thunderstorms, especially in July and August, so take the following precautions.

- Lightning can travel far ahead of a storm, so be sure to take cover before the storm hits.

- Don't try to make it back to your vehicle or campsite. It isn't worth the risk. Instead, seek shelter even if it's only a short way back to the trailhead or camp. Lightning storms usually don't last long, and from a safe vantage point, you might enjoy the sights and sounds.

- Be especially careful not to get caught on a mountaintop or exposed ridge, under large, solitary trees, in the open, or near standing water.

- Seek shelter in a low-lying area, ideally in a dense stand of small, uniformly sized trees.

- Stay away from anything that might attract lightning, such as metal tent poles, graphite fishing rods or trekking poles, or pack frames.

- Get in a crouch position and place both feet firmly on the ground.

Hike early to avoid getting caught exposed in the high country in a thunderstorm.
NATIONAL PARK SERVICE

- Don't walk or huddle together. Instead, stay 50 feet apart, so if somebody gets hit by lightning, others in your party can give first aid.
- If you're in a tent, stay there, in your sleeping bag on your sleeping pad.

HYPOTHERMIA: THE SILENT KILLER

Be aware of the "silent killer," hypothermia, a condition in which the body's internal temperature drops below normal. It can lead to mental and physical collapse, followed shortly by death.

Hypothermia is caused by exposure to cold and is aggravated by wetness, wind, dehydration, and exhaustion. The moment you begin to lose heat faster than your body produces it, you're suffering from exposure. Your body starts involuntary exercise, such as shivering, to stay warm and makes involuntary adjustments to preserve normal temperature in vital organs, restricting blood flow to the extremities. Both responses drain your energy reserves. The only way to stop the drain is to reduce the degree of exposure.

With full-blown hypothermia, as energy reserves are exhausted, cold reaches the brain, depriving you of good judgment and reasoning power. You won't be aware that this is happening. You lose control of your hands. Your internal temperature slides downward. Without treatment, this slide leads to stupor, collapse, and death.

To defend against hypothermia, stay dry. When clothes get wet, they lose most of their insulating value. Wool loses relatively less heat; cotton, down, and some synthetics lose more. Make sure you have quality rain gear that covers head, neck, body, and legs and provides good protection against wind-driven rain. Most hypothermia cases develop in air temperatures between 30 and 50 degrees F, but hypothermia can develop in warmer temperatures, especially when enhanced by dehydration or exhaustion.

If your party is exposed to wind, cold, and wet, automatically think hypothermia. Watch yourself and others for these symptoms: uncontrollable fits of shivering; vague, slow, slurred speech; memory lapses; incoherence; immobile, fumbling hands; frequent stumbling or a lurching gait; drowsiness (to sleep is to die); apparent exhaustion; and inability to get up after a rest. When a member of your party has hypothermia, he or she may deny any problem. Believe the symptoms, not the victim. Even mild symptoms demand treatment, as follows:

- Protect the victim from wind and rain.
- Remove all wet clothing and keep the victim dry.
- Get the victim into warm clothes and a dry sleeping bag.
- Place well-wrapped water bottles filled with heated water close to the victim, especially next to the neck, chest, and groin.
- Try to get the victim to ingest warm liquids, but don't force it.
- Attempt to keep the victim awake.

BE BEAR AWARE

The first step of any hike in bear country is an attitude adjustment. Nothing guarantees total safety. Hiking in bear country such as Grand Teton National Park adds a small additional risk to your trip. That risk can be greatly minimized, however, by adhering to this age-old piece of advice: Be prepared. And being prepared doesn't only mean having the right equipment. It also means having the right information. Knowledge is your best defense.

You can—and should—thoroughly enjoy your trip to bear country. Don't let the fear of bears ruin your experience. This fear can accompany you every step of the way. It can be constantly lurking in the back of your mind, preventing you from enjoying the wildest and most beautiful places left on Earth. And even worse, some bear experts think bears might actually be able to sense your fear.

Being prepared and being knowledgeable gives you confidence. It allows you to fight back the fear that can burden you throughout your stay in bear country. You won't—nor should you—forget about bears and the basic rules of safety, but proper preparation allows you to keep the fear of bears at bay and let enjoyment rule the day.

On top of that, do we really want to be totally safe? If we did, we probably would never go hiking in the wilderness—bears or no bears. We certainly wouldn't, at much greater risk, drive hundreds of miles to get to the trailhead. Perhaps a tinge of danger adds a desired element to our wilderness trip.

HIKING IN BEAR COUNTRY

Nobody likes surprises, and bears dislike them, too. The majority of bear maulings occur when a hiker surprises a bear. Therefore, it's vital to do everything possible to avoid these surprise meetings. Perhaps the best way is to know the five-part system. If you follow these five rules, the chance of encountering a bear on the trail sinks to the slimmest possible margin.

- Be alert.
- Go in with a group and stay together.
- Stay on the trail.
- Hike in the middle of the day.
- Make noise.

No substitute for alertness: As you hike, watch ahead and to the sides. Don't fall into the all-too-common and particularly nasty habit of fixating on the trail 10 feet ahead. It's especially easy to do this when dragging a heavy pack up a long hill or when carefully watching your step on a heavily eroded trail.

Using your knowledge of bear habitat and habits, be especially alert in areas most likely to be frequented by bears, such as avalanche chutes, berry patches, along streams, and through stands of whitebark pine.

Black bears are more common than grizzlies in the park.
NATIONAL PARK SERVICE

Watch carefully for bear signs and be especially watchful (and noisy) if you see any. If you see a track or a scat, but it doesn't look fresh, pretend it's fresh. The area is obviously frequented by bears.

Watch the wind: The wind can be a friend or foe. The strength and direction of the wind can make a significant difference in your chances of an encounter with a bear. When the wind is blowing at your back, your smell travels ahead of you, alerting any bear that might be on or near the trail ahead. Conversely, when the wind blows in your face, your chances of a surprise meeting with a bear increase, so make more noise and be more alert.

A strong wind can also be noisy and limit a bear's ability to hear you coming. If a bear can't smell or hear you coming, the chances of an encounter greatly increase, so watch the wind.

Safety in numbers: There have been very few instances where a large group has had an encounter with a bear. On the other hand, a large percentage of hikers mauled by bears were hiking alone. Large groups naturally make more noise and put out more smell and probably appear more threatening to bears. In addition, if you're hiking alone and get injured, there is nobody to go for help. For these reasons, rangers in Grand Teton recommend parties of four or more hikers when going into bear country.

When a large party splits up, it becomes two small groups and the advantage is lost, so stay together. If you're on a family hike, keep the kids from running ahead. If you're in a large group, keep the stronger members from going ahead or weaker members from lagging behind. The best way to prevent this natural separation is to ask one of the slowest members of the group to lead. This keeps everybody together.

Stay on the trail: Although bears use trails, they don't often use them during midday when hikers commonly use them. Through generations of associating trails with people, bears probably expect to find hikers on trails, especially during midday.

Contrarily, bears probably don't expect to find hikers off trails. Bears rarely settle down in a day bed right along a heavily used trail. If you wander around in thickets off the trail, however, you are more likely to stumble into an occupied day bed or cross paths with a traveling bear.

Sleeping late: Bears—and most other wildlife—usually aren't active during the middle of a day, especially on a hot summer day. Wild animals are most active around dawn and dusk. Therefore, hiking early in the morning or in the late afternoon increases your chances of seeing wildlife, including bears. Likewise, hiking during midday on a hot August day greatly reduces the chance of an encounter.

Sounds: Perhaps the best way to avoid a surprise meeting with a bear is to make sure the bear knows you're coming, so make lots of noise. Some experts think metallic noise is superior to human voices, which can be muffled by natural conditions, but the important issue is making lots of noise, regardless of what kind of noise.

Running: Many avid runners like to get off paved roads and running tracks and onto backcountry trails. But, because of the added element of surprise, running on trails in bear country can be seriously hazardous to your health.

Leave the night to the bears: Like running on trails, hiking at night can be very risky. Bears are more active after dark, and you can't see them until it's too late. If you get caught at night, be sure to make lots of noise, and remember that bears commonly travel on hiking trails at night.

You can be dead meat, too: If you see or smell a carcass of a dead animal when hiking, immediately vacate the area. Don't let your curiosity keep you near the carcass a second longer than necessary. Bears commonly hang around a carcass, guarding it and feeding on it for days until it's completely consumed. Your presence could easily be interpreted as a threat to the bear's food supply, and a vicious attack could be imminent.

If you see a carcass ahead of you on the trail, don't go any closer. Instead, abandon your hike and return to the trailhead. If the carcass is between you and the trailhead, take a very long detour around it, upwind from the carcass, making lots of noise along the way. Be sure to report the carcass to the local ranger. This might prompt a temporary trail closure or special warnings to prevent injury to other hikers. Rangers will, in some cases, go in and drag the carcass away from the trail.

Cute, cuddly, and lethal: If you see a bear cub, don't go 1 inch closer to it. It might seem abandoned, but it most likely is not. Mother bear is probably very close, and female bears fiercely defend their young.

Bear pepper spray: Always carry bear pepper spray. Don't bury it in your pack. Keep it as accessible as possible. Most bear spray comes in a holster or somehow conveniently attaches to your belt or pack. Such protection won't do you any good if you can't have it ready to fire in 1 or 2 seconds. Before hitting the trail, read the directions carefully.

But I didn't see any bears: Now, you know how to be safe. Walk up the trail constantly clanging two metal pans together. It works every time. You won't see a bear, but you might hate your "wilderness experience." You left the city to get away from loud noise.

Yes, you can be very safe, but how safe do you want to be and still be able to enjoy your trip? It's a balancing act. First, be knowledgeable and then decide how far you want to go. Everybody has to make his or her own personal choice.

Here's another conflict. If you do everything listed here, you most likely will not see any bears—or any deer or moose or wolves or any other wildlife. Again, you make the choice. If you want to be as safe as possible, follow these rules religiously. If you want to see wildlife, including bears, do all of the above in reverse, but then remember, you are increasing your chances of an encounter instead of decreasing them.

CAMPING IN BEAR COUNTRY

Staying overnight in bear country is not dangerous, but it adds a slight additional risk to your trip. The main difference is the presence of more food, cooking, and garbage. Plus, you're in bear country at night when bears are usually most active. Once again, however, following a few basic rules greatly minimizes this risk.

Storing food and garbage: Most campsites in Grand Teton have heavy metal, community bear-resistant storage lockers, and you're required to use them. If you're in an

THE BEAR ESSENTIALS OF HIKING AND CAMPING
- Respect any warning signs posted by agencies.
- Knowledge is the best defense.
- There is no substitute for alertness.
- Hike with a large group and stay together.
- Don't hike alone in bear country.
- Don't run trails in bear country.
- Stay on the trail.
- Hike in the middle of the day.
- Carry bear spray; know how to use it; and keep it instantly accessible.
- Make lots of noise while hiking.
- Never approach a bear.
- Stay away from carcasses.
- Separate sleeping and cooking areas.
- Sleep in a tent.
- Cook the right amount of food and eat it all.
- Store food and garbage in metal lockers at campsites or in portable bear-proof containers.
- Never feed bears or let them get unattended food or garbage.
- Keep food odors out of the tent.

off-trail or remote location without a community storage box, the park requires that you keep food in a portable bear-resistant food container. If you don't have your own, the park will rent you one for free with your backcountry permit. Be sure to keep all food and garbage out of reach of bears at all times, day and night.

What to keep in your tent: Do not bring food smells into your tent. Just in case a bear has become accustomed to coming into that campsite looking for food, it's vital to keep all food smells out of the tent. This often includes your pack, which is hard to keep odor-free. Usually only take valuables (like cameras and binoculars), clothing, and sleeping gear into the tent. If you brought a bear pepper spray, sleep with it. Also, keep a flashlight in the tent. If an animal comes into camp and wakes you up, you need the flashlight to identify it.

The campfire: Regulations prohibit campfires in most campsites in Grand Teton, but if you're in an area where fires are allowed, treat yourself. Besides adding the nightly entertainment, the fire might make your camp safer from bears.

The campfire provides the best possible way to get rid of food smells. Build a small but hot fire and thoroughly burn everything that smells of food—garbage, leftovers, fish entrails, everything. If you brought food in cans or other incombustible containers, burn them, too. You can even dump extra water from cooking or dishwater on the edge of the fire to erase the smell.

Be sure to completely burn everything. If you leave partially burned food scraps in the fire, you're setting up a dangerous situation for the next camper to use this site.

Before leaving camp the next morning, dig out the fire pit and pack out anything that has not completely burned, even if you believe it no longer carries food smells. For example, many foods like dried soup or hot chocolate come in foil packages that might seem like they burn, but they really don't. Pack out the scorched foil and cans (now with very minor food smells). Also, pack out foil and cans left by other campers.

Types of food: Don't get paranoid about the types of food you bring. All food has some smell, and you can make your trip much less enjoyable by fretting too much over food.

Perhaps the safest option is freeze-dried food. It carries very little smell, and it comes in convenient envelopes that allow you to "cook it" by merely adding boiling water. This means you don't have cooking pans to wash or store. However, freeze-dried food is very expensive, and many backpackers don't use it—and still safely enjoy bear country.

Dry, pre-packed meals (often pasta- or rice-based) offer an affordable compromise to freeze-dried foods. Also, take your favorite high-energy snack and don't worry about it. Avoid fresh fruit and canned meats and fish.

The key point is: What food you have along is much less critical than how you handle it, cook it, and store it. A can of tuna fish might put out a smell, but if you eat all of it in one meal, don't spill it on the ground or on your clothes, and burn the can later, it can be quite safe.

How to cook: The overriding philosophy of cooking in bear country is to create as little odor as possible. Keep it simple. Use as few pans and dishes as possible. Unless it's a weather emergency, don't cook in the tent. If you like winter backpacking, you might cook in the tent, but you should have a different tent for summer backpacking.

If you can have a campfire and decide to cook fish, try cooking in aluminum foil envelopes instead of frying the fish. Then, after removing the cooked fish, quickly and completely burn the fish scraps off the foil. Using foil also means you don't have to wash the pan you used to cook the fish.

Be careful not to spill on yourself while cooking. If you do, change clothes and store the dirty clothes with the food and garbage. Wash your hands thoroughly before retiring to the tent.

Don't cook too much food, so you don't have to deal with leftovers. If you do end up with extra food, however, you have only two choices: Carry it out or burn it. Don't bury it or throw it in a lake or leave it anywhere in bear country. A bear will most likely find and dig up any food or garbage buried in the backcountry.

Taking out the garbage: In bear country, you have only two choices—burn garbage or carry it out. Prepare for garbage problems before you leave home. Bring along airtight zip-lock bags to store garbage. Be sure to safely store your garbage at night along with your food in metal food lockers. Also, carry in as little garbage as possible by discarding excess packaging while packing.

Washing dishes: This is a sticky problem, but there is one easy solution. If you don't dirty dishes, you don't have to wash them. So try to minimize food smell by using as few dishes and pans as possible—and wash the ones you do use as soon as you finish with them. If you use the principles of no-trace camping, you are probably doing as much as you can to reduce food smell from dishes.

If you brought paper towels, use one to carefully remove food scraps from pans and dishes before washing them. Then, when you wash dishes, you have much less food smell. Burn the dirty towels or store them in zip-lock bags with other garbage. Put pans and dishes in zip-lock bags before putting them back in your pack.

If you end up with lots of food scraps in the dishwater, drain out the scraps and store them in zip-lock bags with other garbage or burn them. You can bring a lightweight screen to filter out food scraps from dishwater, but be sure to store the screen with the food and garbage. If you have a campfire, pour the dishwater around the edge of the fire. If you don't have a fire, take the dishwater at least 200 feet downwind and downhill from camp and pour it on the ground or in a small hole. Don't put dishwater or food scraps in a lake or stream.

Although possibly counter to accepted rules of cleanliness for many people, you can skip washing dishes altogether on the last night of your backpacking trip. Instead, simply use the paper towels to clean the dirty dishes as much as possible. You can wash them when you get home. Pack dirty dishes in zip-lock bags before putting them back in your pack.

During your hike, however, don't put it off. Do dishes immediately after eating, so a minimum of food smell lingers in the area.

Choosing a tent site: Try to keep your tent site at least 100 feet from your cooking area. In Grand Teton, unfortunately, some campsites don't adequately separate the cooking area from the tent site. Store food at least 100 yards from the tent in a portable canister or community locker. You can store it near the cooking area to further concentrate food smells.

Do somebody a big favor: Report all bear encounters to the ranger after your trip. This might not help you, but it could save another camper's life. If rangers get enough reports to spot a pattern, they can manage the area to prevent potentially hazardous situations.

BE MOUNTAIN LION AWARE, TOO

The most important safety tip for hiking in mountain lion country, like Grand Teton National Park, is simply recognizing the habitat. Mountain lions primarily feed on deer, so when you see a lot of deer, you're more likely to see a mountain lion, too.

SAFETY GUIDELINES FOR TRAVELING IN MOUNTAIN LION COUNTRY

To stay as safe as possible when hiking in mountain lion country, follow this advice.

- Travel with a friend or group. There's safety in numbers, so stay together.
- Never let small children wander away by themselves or hike ahead or behind adult hiking companions.

- Avoid hiking at dawn and dusk—the times mountain lions are most active.
- Know how to behave if you encounter a mountain lion.

WHAT TO DO IF YOU ENCOUNTER A MOUNTAIN LION

The vast majority of mountain lion encounters don't result in an injury, so try to keep your cool and consider the following:

Recognize threatening mountain lion behavior. If the lion is more than 50 yards away and it directs its attention to you, it may be only curious. This situation represents only a slight risk for adults, but a more serious risk to unaccompanied children. Move away, keeping the animal in your peripheral vision, while looking for rocks, sticks, or something to use as a weapon, just in case.

If a mountain lion is crouched and staring intensely at you less than 50 yards away, it may be assessing the chances of a successful attack. If this behavior continues, an attack may follow. Here is what you should and should not do:

- Don't approach the lion. Instead, give the animal the opportunity to move on.
- Slowly back away, but maintain eye contact if close.
- Grab the kids.
- Don't run; running may stimulate a predatory response.
- Make noise.
- Continue to maintain eye contact as you move away.
- Be as large and threatening as possible. Raise your arms above your head and make steady waving motions. Raise your jacket or another object above your head. Band together into one group to look larger and more threatening.
- Don't bend over; it makes you appear smaller and "preylike."
- If attacked, defend yourself. Try to remain standing. Don't "play dead." Fight back any way you can with any weapon you can find.
- Defend others, too, but don't defend your pet.
- Report all encounters to local rangers.

TETON VILLAGE AREA

Grand Teton from the Cascade Canyon
Trail, part of the Teton Crest route
NATIONAL PARK SERVICE

1 PHELPS LAKE

WHY GO?

A short day hike or easy overnighter to a popular low-elevation lake.

THE RUNDOWN

Start: Whitegrass/Death Canyon Trailhead
Distance: 4.0-mile out and back
Difficulty: Easy
Nat Geo TOPO! Map (USGS): Grand Teton

Nat Geo Trails Illustrated Map: Grand Teton National Park
Other maps: Earth Walk Press Grand Teton map; NPS handout map

FINDING THE TRAILHEAD

The trailhead is called Whitegrass on some maps and signs and Death Canyon on others, but it's the same place. From Jackson, take WY 22 west for 6 miles to the Moose-Wilson Road junction, just before entering the small town of Wilson. Turn right (north) here, go past Teton Village into the park, and continue on this road (which turns to gravel) until you see the Death Canyon Trailhead turnoff on your left (west), 11.5 miles from WY 22. If you're coming from the north, the trailhead is 3.1 miles south of the Moose Visitor Center on Moose-Wilson Road, which turns south right across from the visitor center and doesn't go through the entrance station. After turning off Moose-Wilson Road, drive 1.6 miles to the actual trailhead, the last mile of which is an unpaved road that can get rough. The Park Service recommends a high-clearance vehicle for this road. The trailhead has toilet facilities and a fairly large parking area, but this trailhead is so popular that it's often full, especially at midday. **GPS:** 43.656039 / -110.781367

THE HIKE

Phelps Lake, a low-elevation lake, is one of the most popular destinations in the park. It's an easy day outing, but also an ideal place for the new backpacker to try that first night in the wilderness.

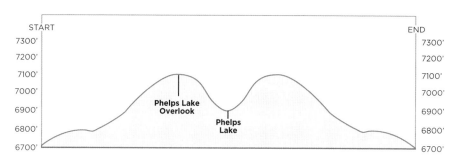

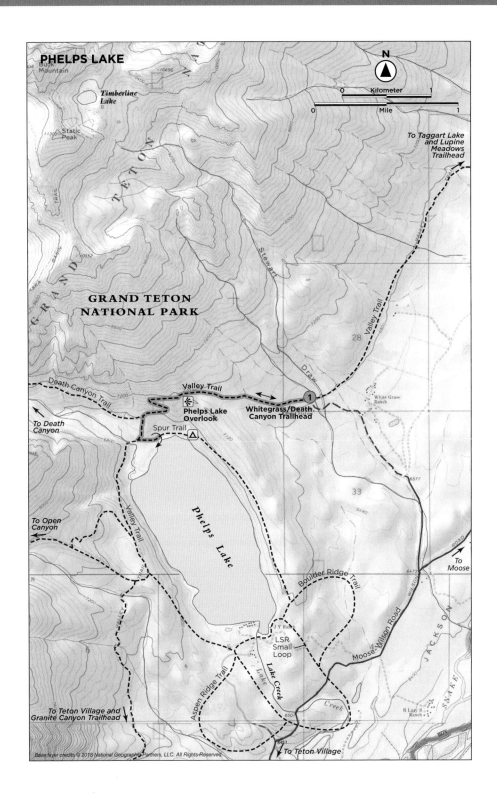

PHELPS LAKE

Bivouac
Mountain

Timberline
Lake

Static
Peak

GRAND TETON
NATIONAL PARK

To Taggart Lake
and Lupine
Meadows
Trailhead

N

0   Kilometer   1

0   Mile   1

Stewart

Valley Trail

White Grass
Ranch

Death Canyon Trail

Valley Trail

Phelps Lake
Overlook

Whitegrass/Death
Canyon Trailhead

To Death
Canyon

Spur Trail

To Open
Canyon

Valley Trail

Phelps Lake

Boulder Ridge Trail

To
Moose

JACKSON

Moose-Wilson Road

J Y Ranch

LSR
Small
Loop

SNAKE

Lake Creek

Aspen Ridge Trail

Creek

R Lazy S
Ranch

To Teton Village and
Granite Canyon Trailhead

To Teton Village

Phelps Lake is on the Valley Trail, which goes from Teton Village to the Lupine Meadows Trailhead. You can reach it from several trailheads, but the shortest, most popular route starts at the Death Canyon Trailhead (called Whitegrass Trailhead on some maps and signs).

Only 0.1 mile after leaving the trailhead parking lot, you reach the first junction with the Valley Trail. Go left (southwest) and hike 0.8 mile up a gradual hill to the Phelps Lake Overlook, where you get a nice view of the lake and the valley beyond.

From here it's a steep downhill on switchbacks to Phelps Lake with a left (south) turn at the junction with the trail up Death Canyon. If you're camping, take a left on a spur trail just as you get to the lake instead of following the Valley Trail along the west side of the lake.

The well-maintained trail goes through mature forest most of the way, with one brush-covered open slope above Phelps Lake. Watch for moose and black bears, which are commonly seen around the lake. Enjoy some fishing (with a Wyoming state fishing license) for brook, cutthroat, and lake trout. After your stay at Phelps Lake, retrace your steps back to the trailhead, keeping in mind that the way back involves a fairly steep climb up to the Phelps Lake Overlook.

Camping: Phelps Lake has three excellent campsites. As you approach the lake, watch for a junction with a trail going to the left (east) to the campsites. All three are on the lake's north shore with a good view of the lake, fire pits, and room for two tents. Two share a food storage box; one has its own. The campsites are out of sight of the main trail,

Enjoying Phelps Lake

Thousands of hikers enjoy this view of Phelps Lake every year.

but they are fairly close. Please talk softly to respect the privacy of others. Campsite GPS: 43.652799 / –110.79865, 43.652406 / –110.797630, 43.65191 / –110.796900

Option: You can make this a shuttle by leaving a vehicle at the Granite Canyon Trailhead, which would make this a 6.1-mile hike.

MILES AND DIRECTIONS

0.0   Whitegrass/Death Canyon Trailhead.

0.1   Junction with Valley Trail; turn left.

0.9   Phelps Lake Overlook.

1.6   Junction with Death Canyon Trail; turn left.

2.0   Phelps Lake; turn around and retrace your route.

4.0   Whitegrass/Death Canyon Trailhead.

2 LSR PRESERVE SMALL LOOP

WHY GO?

An easy and popular day hike to a low-elevation lake.

THE RUNDOWN

Start: Laurance S. Rockefeller Preserve Interpretive Center
Distance: 3.0-mile loop
Difficulty: Easy
Nat Geo TOPO! Map (USGS): Grand Teton

Nat Geo Trails Illustrated Map: Grand Teton National Park
Other maps: Earth Walk Press Grand Teton map; LSR Trail Guide, available free at the trailhead

FINDING THE TRAILHEAD

Drive north of Teton Village on Moose-Wilson Road for 4.4 miles, turn right (east) into the Laurance S. Rockefeller Preserve, and drive 0.5 mile more to the parking area. Since parking space is limited by design to minimize the environmental impact, park close to other vehicles to free up as many spaces as possible. The parking area has a high-tech composting toilet with running water. The parking lot usually fills up by 11 a.m. No overnight parking is allowed. **GPS:** 43.626403 / -110.775381

THE HIKE

The Laurance S. Rockefeller Preserve (LSR Preserve) has a small but expertly designed system of trails that connect with long-established trails outside the preserve in the park, providing hikers with several options for loop hikes. I've included two—one short and one long—in this book, but you can easily modify these routes to fit with your ambitions for the day.

The LSR Preserve officially opened to the public in June 2008, and it's all about returning what had previously been private land to the American people and restoring wild nature to the greatest extent possible while allowing all of us the opportunity to experience it. From 2004 to 2007, thirty buildings plus multiple roads and utilities were removed from the 1,106-acre preserve and the sites reclaimed. In the parking lot, two of the best spaces are reserved for hybrid vehicles. You won't find paper towels or lights in the bathroom, and there are no trash cans in the parking lot. This is, according to the NPS, a Leave No Trace facility, so you must pack out what you pack in, and that includes in the parking lot. Even the trail signs are knee high to make them minimally obtrusive. Unlike many other park trails, horses are prohibited on LSR Preserve trails.

This 3-mile loop up one side and down the other side of Lake Creek, the outlet of Phelps Lake, is the primary hike in the LSR Preserve and the one most often used for

The main LSR trail follows Lake Creek.

ranger-guided hikes. If you're interested in a guided trip, call the interpretive center in advance (307-739-3654) to check on the schedule and availability.

This entire route is well defined and heavily used, so expect to see a lot of people out enjoying the preserve. All stream crossings have sturdy bridges, and there's even a modern composting toilet at Phelps Lake.

You can take the loop clockwise or counterclockwise with no change in difficulty, but this description follows the clockwise option.

After taking the short walk from the parking lot to the interpretive center, you'll find the trailhead on the west side of the spiffy, "bright green" building. I call it that because the interpretive center is the first platinum-level Leadership in Energy and Environmental Design (LEED)–certified building ever constructed in the National Park System.

After 0.1 mile, you can stop at two platforms, one constructed over Lake Creek and another at the base of a small waterfall on a Lake Creek tributary coming in from the north. Shortly after these viewpoints, the trail forks. Go left (southwest) on the Lake Creek Trail, which closely follows the cascading mountain stream most of the way to Phelps Lake. At the junction with the Aspen Ridge Trail and the connecting trail to the Woodland Trail, go straight.

At the lake, you'll find an idyllic viewpoint with benches, perfect for relaxing and soaking in the view of Albright Peak and Rendezvous Mountain as they reflect in Phelps Lake, definitely one of the most spectacular vistas in Grand Teton National Park.

The view from the rest area on the shore of Phelps Lake

From here, the trail follows the lakeshore for about a half-mile, crossing Lake Creek on the nicest bridge I've ever seen, complete with benches beckoning you to stop and enjoy it instead of simply crossing and leaving it behind. Also, you can take one of several short spur trails down to the lakeshore and find a private spot to savor the scenic splendor and allow the wild essence of the place to take root in your consciousness.

When you reach the junction with the Woodland Trail, turn right (southeast). From here, the trail drops gradually all the way back to the interpretive center. If you didn't stop to see the fantastic interpretive displays before you started the hike, be sure to take time to check them out before heading back to the parking lot. The NPS staffs the interpretive center with rangers eager to answer any questions you might have.

Before you drive away, take a moment to think how fortunate we are that Laurance S. Rockefeller decided to donate this amazing place to the park for the enjoyment of future generations instead of selling it for many millions to a developer. Let's hope this idea catches on among the super rich.

Options: You have several options for lengthening your trip. You can add the 4-mile loop around Phelps Lake (Distance, 9 miles). You can also add the Aspen Ridge Loop (Distance, 4.6 miles) or the Boulder Ridge Loop (Distance, 3.9 miles)—or both, of course.

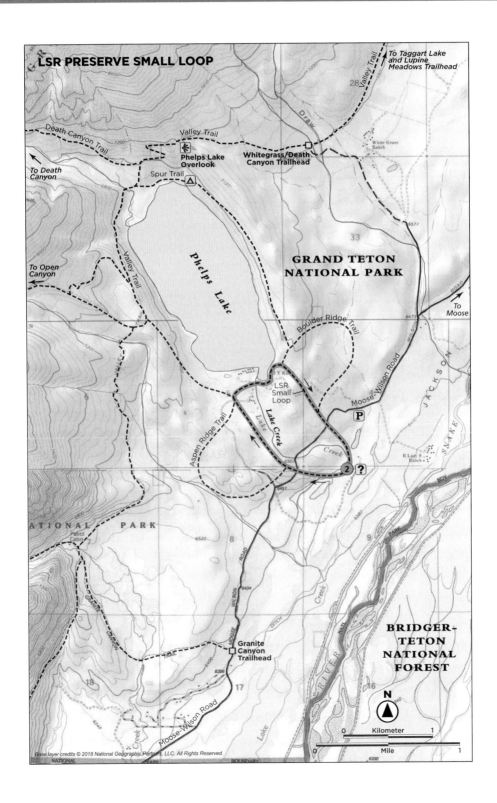

LSR PRESERVE SMALL LOOP

To Taggart Lake
and Lupine
Meadows Trailhead

Valley Trail

28

Draw

Death Canyon Trail

7200

Valley Trail

Phelps Lake
Overlook

Whitegrass/Death
Canyon Trailhead

White Grass
Ranch

To Death
Canyon

Spur Trail

6577

33

GRAND TETON
NATIONAL PARK

To Open
Canyon

Valley Trail

Phelps Lake

6473

To
Moose

Boulder Ridge Trail

N

LSR
Small
Loop

JACKSON

Moose-Wilson Road

P

Aspen Ridge Trail

Lake Creek

SNAKE

R Lazy S
Ranch

2 ?

NATIONAL PARK

Patrol
Cabin

6520

8

Creek

9

BOY

WILSON ROAD

6434

DITCH

Creek

RIVER

MNT

PARK

BRIDGER-
TETON
NATIONAL
FOREST

Granite
Canyon
Trailhead

6388

17

16

N

Moose-Wilson Road

Kilometer   1

Mile   1

This sign in the LSR Preserve parking lot gives you a clue of the guiding philosophy of this "new wilderness."

MILES AND DIRECTIONS

0.0   Laurance S. Rockefeller Interpretive Center.

0.1   Trail splits; turn left onto Lake Creek Trail.

0.6   Cross Moose-Wilson Road.

0.7   Junction with Aspen Ridge Trail and connecting trail to Woodland Trail; go straight.

1.5   Phelps Lake and junction with Aspen Ridge Trail; turn right.

1.7   Toilet.

1.8   Lake Creek.

1.9   Junction with Phelps Lake Trail; turn right onto Woodland Trail.

2.3   Junction with Boulder Ridge Trail and connecting trail to Lake Creek Trail; go straight.

2.6   Moose-Wilson Road.

2.9   Junction with Lake Creek Trail; turn left.

3.0   Laurance S. Rockefeller Interpretive Center.

3 LSR PRESERVE BIG LOOP

WHY GO?
A moderate day hike or overnighter through the LSR and around Phelps Lake.

FINDING THE TRAILHEAD
Drive north of Teton Village on Moose-Wilson Road for 4.4 miles, turn right (east) into the Laurance S. Rockefeller Preserve, and drive 0.5 mile more to the parking area. Since parking space is limited, park close to other vehicles to free up as many spaces as possible. The parking area has a high-tech composting toilet with running water. The parking lot usually fills up by 11 a.m. No overnight parking is allowed, which means backpackers starting at this trailhead will need to be dropped off and picked up at the end of their hike. **GPS:** 43.626403 / -110.775381

THE HIKE
The Laurance S. Rockefeller Preserve (LSR Preserve) has a small maze of trails that connect with the north-south running Valley Trail on the east slope of the Teton Range. Combine the LSR Preserve trails with the park's long-established trails, and you can make an amazing loop hike.

From the trailhead on the west side of the LSR Interpretive Center, go 0.1 mile, past two great viewpoints, to a fork in the trail. You can take this route either clockwise or counterclockwise, but this description follows the clockwise option, so turn left (southwest) here.

You cross Moose-Wilson Road and continue following Lake Creek for another 0.1 mile to the junction with the Aspen Ridge Trail. Turn left (south) here and take the 2.5-mile loop trail to Phelps Lake. The trail climbs over a small ridge with, of course, groves of aspen, down to follow Kaufman Creek for about a half-mile before heading up over the ridge again and down to Phelps Lake and the junction with the loop trail around the lake.

After relaxing at the viewpoint at this junction with its postcard views of Albright Peak and Rendezvous Mountain reflecting in the lake, head around the lake. The trail closely follows the lakeshore, going over a big bog on a new metal-mesh walkway, past Huckleberry Point (a must-do side trip), and then climbs gradually away from the lake-shore up to the Valley Trail.

And yes, there are huckleberries, but you'll probably have to wait until August for them to ripen.

Turn right (north) on the Valley Trail and right (northeast) again 0.4 mile later and then back down to the shoreline of Phelps Lake. You come out at the west-shore beach where you might see people swimming and sunbathing. Shortly down the trail, you pass the three designated Phelps Lake campsites.

The west side of Phelps Lake along the Valley Trail has a great abundance of wildflow-ers, and possibly because of the fertility of the area, they tend to grow larger than usual.

The trail on the north shore of the lake stays farther away from the shoreline than the south-shore trail, but still offers stunning views of the lake and Rendezvous Mountain. Just before you reach the end of the lake, turn left (northeast) onto the Boulder Ridge Trail.

Only 0.1 mile or less up the Boulder Ridge Trail, check out David Spalding's grave-stone on your left. Spalding homesteaded here in 1903, but after a few years of struggling to eke out a livelihood, he gave up and sold out to Louis Joy. Later it became the JY Guest Ranch and was then sold to John D. Rockefeller Jr., who passed it on to his son,

Phelps Lake and
Rendezvous Mountain

Hiking the Aspen Ridge
Trail in the LSR Preserve

Laurance. The Rockefellers operated it as a private retreat for 70 years before donating it to Grand Teton National Park.

Halfway around the Boulder Ridge Trail, it splits. You can take either the high or low trail; they join up 0.2 mile later. The upper trail (left) is in better shape and offers the best scenery, but the lower trail weaves through a huge boulder field that gave the trail its name.

After another 0.5 mile, you come to the Woodland Trail. Turn left (east) here and follow it back to the interpretive center.

Interesting side note: We saw a hundred or more people hiking the Lake Creek and Woodland Trails, but not a single hiker on the Boulder Ridge or Aspen Ridge Trails, even though they were at least as nice.

Laurance S. Rockefeller wanted to manage the preserve as a natural area with a careful balance between preservation and public access. After taking this remarkable loop hike, it would be hard to argue that he didn't get exactly what he wanted.

Side trip: You'll be sorry if you miss the short (0.2 mile total) side trip out to Huckleberry Point.

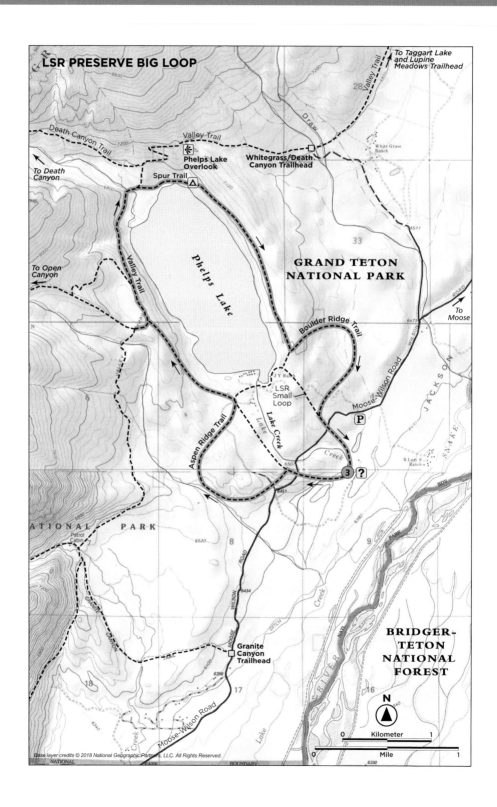

LSR PRESERVE BIG LOOP

To Taggart Lake and Lupine Meadows Trailhead

Valley Trail

Draw

28

White Grass Ranch

Death Canyon Trail

7200

Valley Trail

Phelps Lake Overlook

Whitegrass/Death Canyon Trailhead

To Death Canyon

Spur Trail

33

GRAND TETON NATIONAL PARK

To Open Canyon

Valley Trail

Phelps Lake

Boulder Ridge Trail

To Moose

JACKSON

J Y Ranch

LSR Small Loop

Moose-Wilson Road

Aspen Ridge Trail

Lake Creek

P

3 ?

R Lazy S Ranch

SNAKE

Lake

Creek

NATIONAL PARK

Patrol Cabin

6520

8

9

BRIDGER-TETON NATIONAL FOREST

GRANITE CANYON TRAIL

Moose-Wilson Road

Granite Canyon Trailhead

17

16

N

Kilometer   1

Mile   1

Camping: Make this a moderate overnighter by getting a permit for one of three excellent campsites at Phelps Lake. All three campsites are on a small ridge about 200 feet above the lake to ensure privacy. Of the three, campsite 3 is probably the nicest with the best view and its own food area and bear box. Campsites 1 and 2 share the same food area and bear box. Remember, no overnight camping at the LSR Preserve parking lot.

MILES AND DIRECTIONS

0.0	Laurance S. Rockefeller Interpretive Center.
0.1	Trail splits; turn left onto Lake Creek Trail.
0.6	Cross Moose-Wilson Road.
0.7	Junction with Aspen Ridge Trail; turn left.
3.2	Phelps Lake and the junction with Phelps Lake Trail; turn left.
3.8	Huckleberry Point spur trail; go left.
5.0	Junction with Valley Trail; turn right.
5.4	Junction with Death Canyon Trail; turn right.
7.0	Junction with Boulder Ridge Trail; turn left.
7.1	David Spalding grave.
7.5	Junction with Boulder Ridge loop; turn left.
7.7	Junction with Boulder Ridge loop; turn left.
8.3	Junction with Woodland Trail; turn left.
8.6	Moose-Wilson Road.
8.9	Junction with Lake Creek Trail; turn left.
9.0	Laurance S. Rockefeller Interpretive Center.

4 **MARION LAKE**

WHY GO?
A long, hard day hike or moderate overnighter to a high-elevation lake.

THE RUNDOWN
Start: Top of tram at Teton Village
Distance: 14.7-mile lollipop loop
Difficulty: Difficult day hike; moderate overnighter
Nat Geo TOPO! Map (USGS): Teton Village

Nat Geo Trails Illustrated Map: Grand Teton National Park
Other maps: Earth Walk Press Grand Teton map; NPS handout map

FINDING THE TRAILHEAD
Take the tram behind the main ski lodge in Teton Village to the top of Rendezvous Mountain to start this hike. Teton Village is 12.5 miles northwest of Jackson. From Jackson, take WY 22 west for about 6 miles to the Moose-Wilson Road junction, just before the small town of Wilson. Turn right (north), go 6.5 miles, and turn left (west) into Teton Village. Park in the main ski lodge parking lot. Teton Village has restaurants, shopping, and toilet facilities in the lodge. **GPS:** 43.587517 / -110.827183

AUTHOR'S NOTE: When I originally wrote this book in 1998, the cost of using the Teton Village Tram was nicely affordable, so I recommended taking the short tram ride to the top of Rendezvous Mountain to start this hike. The ride saves hikers time, a few miles of extra hiking, and a healthy climb. Since then, the tram's owners have significantly increased the cost of the tram ride to $42 per adult, as I write this note in 2017, with some small discounts for children and for booking online in advance. This means that a group of five adults would have to fork over $200 just to get to the trailhead. Because of this unrealistic cost and the likelihood that it will continue to soar, I'll be rewriting all the hikes in a future revision to skip the tram ride. In the meantime, if you think the cost is too high, you can get out a map and easily see how you can access the same trails on foot from the Valley or Granite Trailheads.

THE HIKE
Marion Lake is a long day hike, but you can start it the easy way, going downhill, if you take the tram from Teton Village. You could hike 6.6 miles up to the top of 10,450-foot Rendezvous Mountain on the service road instead of taking the tram, but, obviously, that isn't a popular option. The tram leaves every 15 minutes 9 a.m. to 7:30 p.m. with a fee to

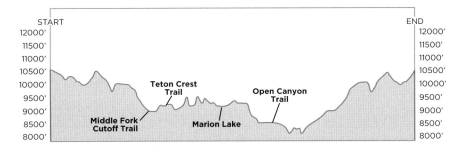

After getting off the tram, hike down a steep ridgeline to the junction with the tram service road and the park boundary. Take this first leg of your trip slowly so you can soak in the incredible view of the Teton Range to the north—including Grand Teton peeping over the skyline—and the valley to the south.

go up but no fee to go down. The Marion Lake hike makes a nice 2-day outing, with a pleasant overnight stay at one of the few mountain lakes in the park.

Be sure to take a map. This route has a lot of junctions, and one lapse in concentration could result in getting on the wrong trail. In August and September, this route can be dry, as several intermittent streams dry up, so carry plenty of water. Horses are not allowed on the first 3.9 miles of this trail.

After getting off the tram, hike down a steep ridgeline to the junction with the tram service road and the park boundary. Take this first leg of your trip slowly so you can soak in the incredible view of the Teton Range to the north—including Grand Teton peeping over the skyline—and the valley to the south.

At the park boundary, turn right (west) and take one big switchback down the steep slope of Rendezvous Mountain into a bowl. You can see the trail heading up on the other side of the bowl. After the descent through some talus and subalpine vegetation, you move into spruce forest interspersed with large meadows. Most of the rest of the trail goes through this type of terrain.

When you get to the next junction at Middle Fork Cutoff Trail, you can take the loop in either direction, but this hike describes the clockwise route, so take a left (west) at this junction and right (north) at the next two junctions at the Teton Crest Trail (to Moose Creek Pass) and Game Creek, until you drop down into the North Fork of Granite Creek below Marion Lake. From there, you are treated with a short but steep climb up to the lake.

Marion Lake is a little jewel tucked in the shadow of mighty Housetop Mountain and surrounded by wildflower-carpeted meadows. Even if you aren't staying overnight, plan on spending some serious time at the lake. It's too nice to view quickly and then abandon. But don't dawdle too long. Unless you're spending the night, you have to make it back before 7:30 p.m. to catch the last tram.

After a rest or lunch break or overnight stay at the lake, drop back down into the North Fork, but this time turn left (east) and go down the North Fork of Granite Creek. Most of this leg of the trip goes through a giant meadow on the north side of the stream. At the junction with the Open Canyon Trail to the Mount Hunt Divide, veer right (east) through an open forest to the Middle Fork Cutoff Trail. Turn right (south) and go through another huge meadow back to the Rendezvous Mountain Trail junction you passed earlier in your trip. From here go left (east) and retrace your steps back to the tram.

Marion Lake
NATIONAL PARK SERVICE

Save some energy and water for the last pitch up to the tram. It can be a tough finish, especially on a hot day, to a great hike.

Camping: Marion Lake has three heavily used campsites with a good water source and nice views (although you can only see the lake from the first campsite and then just

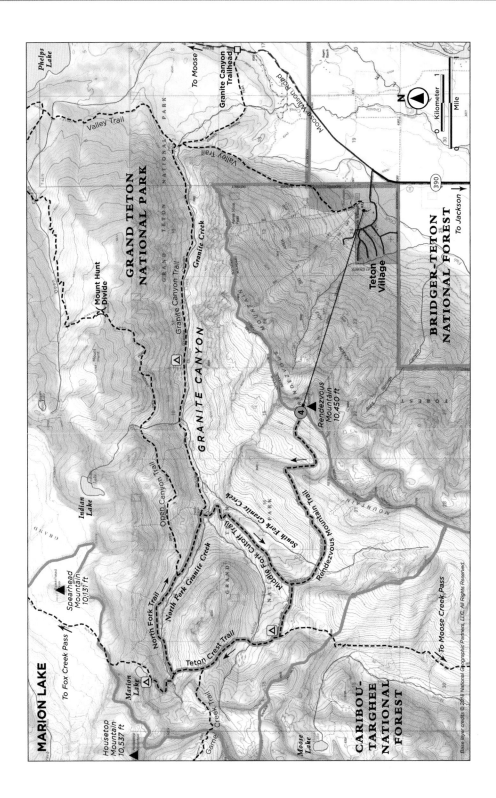

MARION LAKE

Housetop Mountain
10,537 ft

CARIBOU-
TARGHEE
NATIONAL
FOREST

Moose Lake

To Moose Creek Pass

Game Creek Trail

Teton Crest Trail

Marion Lake

To Fox Creek Pass

North Fork Trail

North Fork Granite Creek

Middle Fork Cutoff Trail

South Fork Granite Creek

Rendezvous Mountain Trail

Rendezvous Mountain
10,450 ft

4

Open Canyon Trail

Indian Lake

Spearhead Mountain
10,131 ft

GRANITE CANYON

Granite Canyon Trail

Granite Creek

GRAND TETON
NATIONAL PARK

Mount Hunt
Divide

Valley Trail

Phelps Lake

Valley Trail

Granite Canyon
Trailhead

To Moose

Moose-Wilson Road

390

To Jackson

Teton Village

BRIDGER-TETON
NATIONAL FOREST

N

Kilometer

Mile

barely), with two raised tent pads each. You can also camp at the Middle Fork Camping Zone or the Upper Granite Canyon Camping Zone. Upper Granite has nicer campsites along the stream and good water sources. The Middle Fork campsites generally offer better views, but water can be scarce in many areas, especially in late August and September when intermittent streams dry up. Marion Lake has designated campsites, but the two camping zones allow you to find your own campsite.

Options: You can hike the loop in reverse, but you face a fairly steep climb coming out of the South Fork of Granite Creek. You can also hike out and back and cut 1.5 miles off the distance.

Side trips: If you have the time, you can hike about a half-mile up from Marion Lake to a gorgeous high-altitude plateau. You can also take a side trip (about 1.4 miles round-trip from Teton Crest Trail) over to Moose Creek Divide for a great view. The Game Creek Trail more or less ends at the park boundary. Officially it continues on, but it's very difficult to follow. But the stunning view from the boundary, one of the grandest in the park, makes this a great out-and-back side trip.

MILES AND DIRECTIONS

0.0	Top of the Teton Village Tram.
0.4	Junction with tram service road and park boundary; turn right.
3.9	Junction with Middle Fork Cutoff Trail; turn left.
4.4	Junction with Teton Crest Trail (to Moose Creek Pass); turn right.
5.4	Junction with Game Creek Trail; turn right.
6.0	Junction with North Fork Trail; turn left.
6.6	Marion Lake.
7.2	Junction with North Fork Trail; turn left.
8.4	Junction with Open Canyon Trail; turn right.
9.1	Junction with Middle Fork Cutoff Trail; turn right.
10.8	Junction with Rendezvous Mountain Trail; turn left.
13.9	Junction with tram service road; turn left.
14.7	Top of Teton Village Tram.

5 RENDEZVOUS MOUNTAIN AND GRANITE CANYON

WHY GO?

A scenic, mostly downhill route with overnight option.

THE RUNDOWN

Start: Top of the Teton Village Tram
Distance: 12.8-mile loop
Difficulty: Moderate
Nat Geo TOPO! Map (USGS): Teton Village

Nat Geo Trails Illustrated Map: Grand Teton National Park
Other maps: Earth Walk Press Grand Teton map; NPS handout map

FINDING THE TRAILHEAD

Take the tram behind the main ski lodge in Teton Village to the top of Rendezvous Mountain to start this hike. Teton Village is 12.5 miles northwest of Jackson. From Jackson, take WY 22 west for about 6 miles to the Moose-Wilson Road junction, just before the small town of Wilson. Turn right (north), and go 6.5 miles. Turn left (west) into Teton Village. Park in the main ski lodge parking lot. Teton Village has restaurants, shopping, and toilet facilities in the lodge. If you take the shuttle option, leave a vehicle or arrange to be picked up at the Granite Canyon Trailhead, which is 2.1 miles north of Teton Village on Moose-Wilson Road. **GPS:** 43.587517 / -110.827183

AUTHOR'S NOTE: When I originally wrote this book in 1998, the cost of using the Teton Village Tram was nicely affordable, so I recommended taking the short tram ride to the top of Rendezvous Mountain to start this hike. The ride saves hikers time, a few miles of extra hiking, and a healthy climb. Since then, the tram's owners have significantly increased the cost of the tram ride to $42 per adult, as I write this note in 2017, with some small discounts for children and for booking online in advance. This means that a group of five adults would have to fork over $200 just to get to the trailhead. Because of

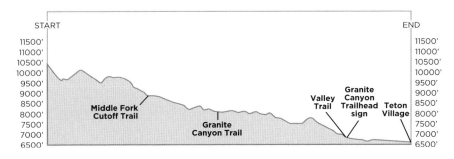

Hiking on top of
Rendezvous Mountain
NATIONAL PARK SERVICE

this unrealistic cost and the likelihood that it will continue to soar, I'll be rewriting all the hikes in a future revision to skip the tram ride. In the meantime, if you think the cost is too high, you can get out a map and easily see how you can access the same trails on foot from the Valley or Granite Trailheads.

THE HIKE

This is the only hike in Grand Teton National Park that starts at the top of a mountain and goes to the valley floor, a perfect choice for hikers who don't like to climb hills. It makes a great day hike or overnighter loop with a good shuttle option.

The trip actually starts in the valley floor at Teton Village at the tramway to the top of Rendezvous Mountain. The tram starts running at 9 a.m. and runs about every 15 minutes until 7:30 p.m. There's a fee to go up, but no fee to go down. The only other option to get to the top of 10,450-foot Rendezvous Mountain is a 6.6-mile climb up the service road.

After getting off the tram, hike down the steep ridgeline to a junction with the tram service road at the park boundary. Take this first leg of your trip slowly so you can soak in the incredible view of the Teton Range to the north, including Grand Teton peeping over the skyline, and the valley to the south.

At the park boundary, turn right (west) and take one big switchback down the steep slope of Rendezvous Mountain into a bowl. You can see the trail heading up on the other side of the bowl (the only hill you'll have to climb on this route). After the descent through some talus and subalpine vegetation, you move into spruce forest interspersed with large meadows. Horses are not allowed on the first 3.9 miles of this trail.

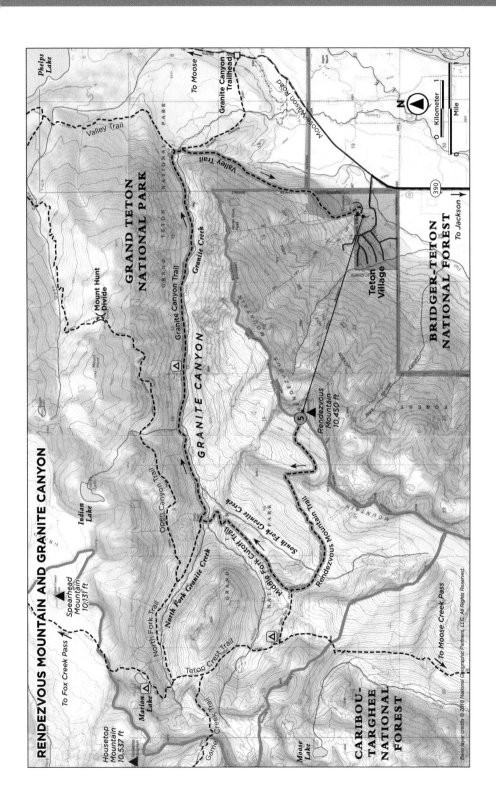

RENDEZVOUS MOUNTAIN AND GRANITE CANYON

Phelps Lake

Valley Trail

To Moose

Granite Canyon Trailhead

Moose-Wilson Road

GRAND TETON NATIONAL PARK

GRAND TETON NATIONAL PARK

Valley Trail

390

To Jackson

Mount Hunt Divide

Granite Canyon Trail

Granite Creek

GRANITE CANYON

Teton Village

BRIDGER–TETON NATIONAL FOREST

Indian Lake

Spearhead Mountain 10,131 ft

Open Canyon Trail

Rendezvous Mountain 10,450 ft

5

Rendezvous Mountain Trail

To Fox Creek Pass

North Fork Trail

Middle Fork Cutoff Trail

South Fork Granite Creek

North Fork Granite Creek

Housetop Mountain 10,537 ft

Marion Lake

Teton Crest Trail

Game Creek Trail

CARIBOU–TARGHEE NATIONAL FOREST

Moose Lake

To Moose Creek Pass

N

Kilometer

Mile

Most of the rest of the trail goes through this type of terrain. In July and early August, expect a spectacular wildflower display in the meadows. In late August and September, this route can be dry, as several intermittent streams dry up, so plan on carrying plenty of water.

When you see the Middle Fork Cutoff junction, go right (north), head through a giant meadow, and drop gradually down to Granite Creek. When you reach the stream, load up on water. Just past the stream is the junction with the Granite Canyon Trail. Go right (east) and start gradually dropping down to the valley floor. The trail stays close to the stream, mostly through meadows in the upper reaches, and becomes gradually more forested as you descend toward the valley floor. The canyon also narrows gradually as you descend. Don't be surprised to meet a group with horses in lower Granite Canyon.

When you reach the junction with the Valley Trail, go right (south) and cross the creek where you'll find another junction (only 0.1 mile down the trail). Go right (south) and follow the Valley Trail to the park boundary and through the ski area back to the main lodge where the tram begins. The trip through the ski area can get confusing, but focus on the tram and you won't get off track.

Camping: You pass through two camping zones with undesignated campsites. The first, the Middle Fork Camping Zone, offers terrific campsites with good views, but water can be scarce later in the summer. The Lower Granite Canyon Camping Zone is mostly in the narrow portion of the canyon, and the best sites are close to the trail with limited privacy but also close to the stream for easy access to water.

Options: You can make this hike with a convenient shuttle. Instead of turning right (south) at the Granite Canyon Trailhead junction, go left (east) and hike 1.5 miles to the Granite Canyon Trailhead. This cuts about 0.9 mile off your trip. You can, of course, take this trip in reverse, but it would be uphill all the way.

MILES AND DIRECTIONS

0.0	Top of the Teton Village Tram.
0.4	Park boundary and junction with tram service road; turn right.
3.9	Junction with Middle Fork Cutoff Trail; turn right.
5.6	Junction with Granite Canyon Trail; turn right.
10.3	Junction with Valley Trail; turn right.
10.4	Junction with trail to Granite Canyon Trailhead; turn right.
12.1	Park boundary.
12.8	Teton Village.

6 DEATH CANYON AND T MOUNT HUNT DIVIDE

WHY GO?

A multi-day backpacking trip through the canyons of the southern section of the park.

THE RUNDOWN

Start: Whitegrass/Death Canyon Trailhead
Distance: 24.2-mile loop
Difficulty: Difficult
Nat Geo TOPO! Map (USGS): Grand Teton

Nat Geo Trails Illustrated Map: Grand Teton National Park
Other maps: Earth Walk Press Grand Teton map; NPS handout map

FINDING THE TRAILHEAD

The trailhead is called Whitegrass on some maps and signs and Death Canyon on others, but it's the same place. From Jackson, take WY 22 west for about 6 miles to the Moose-Wilson Road junction, just before the small town of Wilson. Turn right (north), go past Teton Village and into the park (no entrance station), and continue on this road (which turns to gravel) until you see the Death Canyon Trailhead turnoff on your left (west), 11.5 miles from WY 22. From the north, the trailhead is 3.1 miles south of the Moose Visitor Center on Moose-Wilson Road, which turns south across from the visitor center and doesn't go through the entrance station. After turning off Moose-Wilson Road, drive 1.6 miles to the actual trailhead, the last mile of which is an unpaved road that can get rough. The Park Service recommends a high-clearance vehicle for this road. The trailhead has toilet facilities and a fairly large parking area, but this trailhead is so popular that it can be full, especially at midday. **GPS:** 43.656039 / -110.781367

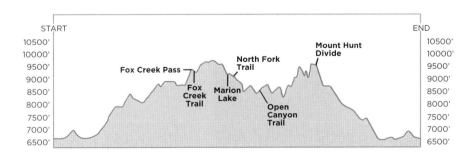

RECOMMENDED ITINERARY: A 3-NIGHT TRIP AS FOLLOWS:

First night: Lower Death Canyon
Second night: Marion Lake
Third night: Phelps Lake

THE HIKE

This multiday route, which goes through three scenic canyons, might lack the popularity of classic backpacking adventures like the Teton Crest and Grand Teton Loop, but it's shorter and less crowded. With a great side trip on the Death Canyon Shelf, you can see one of the better sections of the Teton Crest Trail.

Only 0.1 mile after leaving the trailhead parking lot, you reach the first junction with the Valley Trail. Go left (southwest) and hike 0.8 mile up a gradual hill to the Phelps Lake Overlook, where you get a nice view of the lake and the valley beyond. Phelps Lake is on the Valley Trail, which goes from Teton Village to the Lupine Meadows Trailhead.

Death Canyon
NATIONAL PARK SERVICE

From the overlook, it's a steep downhill on switchbacks to the junction with the Death Canyon Trail just above the lake. If you started late in the day and you're camping at Phelps Lake the first night out, take a left (east) on the Valley Trail, which goes by the lake, but if not, go right (west) and climb into Death Canyon.

The first part of the Death Canyon Trail to the patrol cabin at the junction with the Static Peak Divide Trail is a fairly serious hill. You climb most of the way on a slightly rocky trail along a classic mountain stream cascading out of Death Canyon, which is quite narrow and lined with cliffs most of the way. Like many of the canyons slicing into the Teton Range, the first part is the steepest. Turn around here and there for a nice view of Phelps Lake and Jackson Hole.

At the patrol cabin, the trail levels out for a while and the stream turns smooth in spots. Then the trail gradually ascends all the way to Fox Creek Pass with a very steep last mile. The switchbacks on the pass are short and functional, not those long, nearly level switchbacks that double the distance. Upper Death Canyon becomes gradually more open and scenic as you near the pass. You hike in the shadow of the Death Canyon Shelf to the northwest.

At Fox Creek Pass, you leave the park and enter the Jedediah Smith Wilderness in the Targhee National Forest. Go left (south) at the junction with the trail up the Death Canyon Shelf at the pass. In only 0.1 mile, you hit a somewhat confusing junction (no sign when I was there) with the trail dropping down Fox Creek to the west. Watch the map and be sure to go left (south), and hike along a mostly level plateau for about 2 miles over to Marion Lake. This is a very scenic leg of the hike with massive Housetop Mountain ahead and extremely well-named Spearhead Mountain to the left. When you enter the park again 0.4 mile above Marion Lake, you hike down a steep hill to a small, jewel-like mountain lake you can see all the way down the ridge.

After a stay at Marion Lake, continue steeply downhill for another 0.6 mile until you get to the North Fork of Granite Creek. At the creek bottom, take a left (east) at the junction with the trail going to the South Fork of Granite Creek and to Teton Village. Hike 1.2 miles through the mostly open terrain along the north side of the creek until you reach the Open Canyon Trail to the Mount Hunt Divide.

Go left (northeast) and start hiking the most difficult leg of the trip. The next 4.1 miles go by slowly, as you steadily climb right from the junction up to the Mount Hunt Divide. This tough climb gains about 1,600 feet, and seems long. The terrain fools you, as you think you're "almost there," but it takes much longer than expected. For much of the way, the trail traverses a scenic contour above Granite Canyon.

Mount Hunt Divide (when you finally get there!) offers some spectacular views of the southern Teton Range. You can see Rendezvous Mountain and Apres Vous Peak, which provide the slopes for the Teton Village Ski Area, to the south and most of the big peaks of the Teton Range to the north.

From the divide, the trail drops precipitously down into Open Canyon. You drop through stands of whitebark pine and into a mature lodgepole forest, switchbacking all the way to the creek bottom. Once at the bottom, the trail becomes mostly level as it follows the stream grade down to the Valley Trail.

Go left (east) at the cutoff trail just before you reach the Valley Trail, and left (north) again when you get to the Valley Trail 0.8 mile later. Shortly after getting on the Valley Trail, start hiking the west shore of expansive Phelps Lake. If you plan to camp at the lake, watch for the spur trail to the right taking you around to the three campsites on the north shore. Watch for moose and black bears commonly seen around Phelps Lake. After your stay at the lake, retrace your steps to the trailhead, keeping in mind that the way back involves one last climb up to the Phelps Lake Overlook.

Camping: This is a difficult trip to plan because the Open Canyon and Mount Hunt Camping Zones are probably the least desirable in the park. Having a great campsite is important to me, which is why I recommend doing the 11 tough miles from Marion Lake to Phelps Lake. I camped in the Open Canyon Camping Zone on the east side of

Hiking Death Canyon
NATIONAL PARK SERVICE

the divide, which cut the day's backpack down to 7 or 8 miles. However, I was unhappy with the camping choices in this zone. Ditto for the Mount Hunt Camping Zone I hiked through earlier in the day. Earlier in the year, I had been pleasantly surprised with how much I enjoyed a night at Phelps Lake, so if I did this trip again I'd roll out early from Marion Lake and go all the way to Phelps Lake. You could actually hike all the way out to the trailhead, but this would be almost 13 miles with a big hill—and you'd miss a nice camping experience at Phelps Lake.

The Death Canyon Camping Zone is delightful with its many five-star-indicated campsites, especially in the upper reaches, good access to water, and nice views of the Death Canyon Shelf or Fox Creek Pass. The Death Canyon Shelf Zone is an undesignated camping area, so find a site with a nice view and set up a no-trace camp.

If you spend a night on the shelf, arrange for good weather because it could be ugly on this high, exposed bench during an early-season snowstorm. In August and September, water can get scarce on the shelf, especially in the southern part.

Marion Lake has three designated campsites with two tent pads each. The view is not that spectacular, but it's an easy walk to get water. The sites are about 200 feet from the main trail but fairly close together with limited privacy.

Both the Mount Hunt and Open Canyon Camping Zones offer a poor choice of good campsites, and it's quite difficult to find water late in the season. One basic problem is finding a tent site that's anywhere near level.

Phelps Lake has three excellent designated campsites. As you approach the lake, watch for a junction with a trail going to the right (east) to the campsites. All of them are on the lake's north shore with views of the lake, fire pits, and room for two tents. Two have a shared food storage box; one has its own food area and bear box. The campsites are out of sight of the main trail, but the three campsites are fairly close, so please talk softly to respect the privacy of others.

Options: Add a day to the trip by spending a sure-to-always-be-remembered night on Death Canyon Shelf. If you're interested in this option, turn right (northeast) at Fox Creek Pass and hike 2 to 3 miles along the shelf until you find a five-star campsite (which won't be difficult), then settle in for a memorable night in the high country. In the morning, head over to Marion Lake to your next campsite.

You could, of course, do this trip in reverse, but the Mount Hunt Divide is a monster hill from either side.

Side trips: You would really miss something if you didn't take the side trip out and back on the Death Canyon Shelf—or even better, spend the night.

MILES AND DIRECTIONS

0.0	Whitegrass/Death Canyon Trailhead.
0.1	Junction with Valley Trail; turn left.
0.9	Phelps Lake Overlook.
1.6	Junction with Death Canyon Trail; turn right.

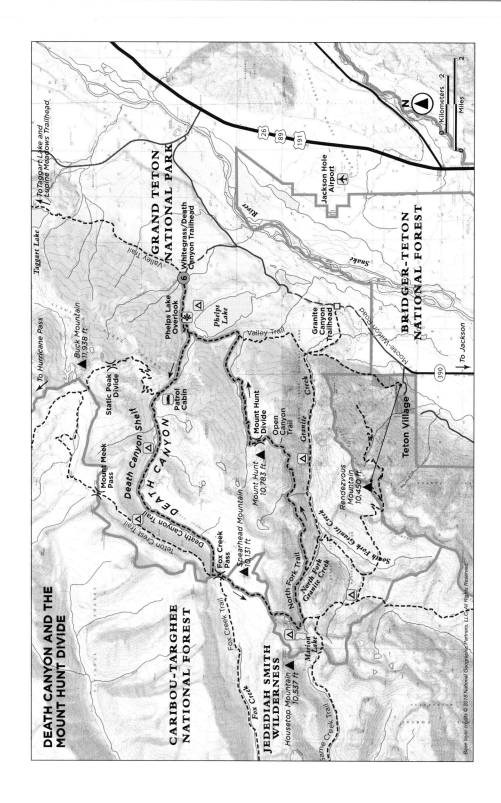

DEATH CANYON AND THE
MOUNT HUNT DIVIDE

GRAND TETON
NATIONAL PARK

BRIDGER-TETON
NATIONAL FOREST

CARIBOU-TARGHEE
NATIONAL FOREST

JEDEDIAH SMITH
WILDERNESS

To Taggart Lake and
Lupine Meadows Trailhead

Taggart Lake

Valley Trail

To Hurricane Pass

Buck Mountain
11,938 ft

Static Peak
Divide

Mount Meek
Pass

Death Canyon Shelf

Teton Crest Trail

Death Canyon Trail

DEATH CANYON

Patrol Cabin

Phelps Lake Overlook

Phelps Lake

Whitegrass/Death
Canyon Trailhead

Valley Trail

Mount Hunt
Divide

Open
Canyon Trail

Granite Creek

Granite Canyon
Trailhead

Teton Village

Rendezvous
Mountain
10,450 ft

Mount Hunt
10,783 ft

Spearhead Mountain
10,131 ft

Fox Creek
Pass

Fox Creek Trail

Fox Creek

North Fork Trail

North Fork
Granite Creek

South Fork Granite Creek

Marion
Lake

Housetop Mountain
10,537 ft

Game Creek Trail

Jackson Hole
Airport

Snake River

Moose-Wilson Road

To Jackson

390

26
89
191

N

Kilometers 2

Miles

Death Canyon as seen from Static Peak
NATIONAL PARK SERVICE

3.7 Patrol cabin and junction with trail to Static Peak Divide; turn left.

9.2 Fox Creek Pass and park boundary.

9.2 Junction with Death Canyon Shelf Trail; turn left.

9.3 Junction with Fox Creek Trail; turn left.

11.1 Park boundary.

11.5 Marion Lake.

12.1 Junction with North Fork Trail; turn left.

13.3 Junction with Open Canyon Trail; turn left.

17.4 Mount Hunt Divide.

20.8 Junction with cutoff trail to Granite Canyon; turn left.

21.6 Junction with Valley Trail; turn left.

22.2 Phelps Lake.

22.6 Junction with Death Canyon Trail; turn right.

23.3 Phelps Lake Overlook.

24.1 Junction with trail to Death Canyon Trailhead; turn right.

24.2 Whitegrass/Death Canyon Trailhead.

THE TETON CREST

WHY GO?

It really doesn't get much better than this, a truly spectacular backpacking adventure starting at 10,450 feet, definitely one of the best in North America.

THE RUNDOWN

Start: Top of tram at Teton Village
Distance: 35.4-mile shuttle
Difficulty: Difficult
Nat Geo TOPO! Map (USGS): Teton Village

Nat Geo Trails Illustrated Map: Grand Teton National Park
Other maps: Earth Walk Press Grand Teton map; NPS handout map

FINDING THE TRAILHEAD

For the shuttle, leave a vehicle at the Leigh Lake Trailhead at the String Lake Picnic Area (GPS: 43.784082 / -110.727354). To find this trailhead, take US 89 north of Jackson for 11.5 miles and turn left (west) at the Moose Junction. Drive past the Moose Visitor Center and through the entrance station (about a mile after turning off the highway). Follow this paved park road for another 9.7 miles from the entrance station to the Jenny Lake turnoff. Turn left (west) and drive 0.6 mile (follow the signs and take two right turns) to the String Lake Trailhead and 0.3 mile farther to the String Lake Picnic Area. The Leigh Lake Trailhead is in the northwest corner of the picnic area. From the north, drive 9.9 miles from the Jackson Lake Junction and turn right (west) at the Jenny Lake turnoff. There are toilet facilities in the picnic area at the Leigh Lake Trailhead.

To start the hike, take the tramway behind the main ski lodge in Teton Village to the top of Rendezvous Mountain. Teton Village is 12.5 miles northwest of Jackson. From Jackson, take WY 22 west for about 6 miles to the Moose-Wilson Road junction, just before the small town of Wilson. Turn right (north), go 6.5 miles, and turn left (west) into Teton Village. Park in the main ski lodge parking lot. **GPS:** 43.587517 / -110.827183

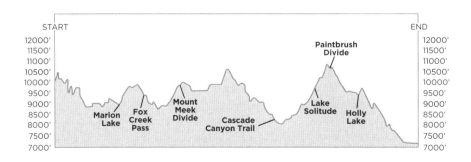

AUTHOR'S NOTE: When I originally wrote this book in 1998, the cost of using the Teton Village Tram was nicely affordable, so I recommended taking the short tram ride to the top of Rendezvous Mountain to start this hike. The ride saves hikers time, a few miles of extra hiking, and a healthy climb. Since then, the tram's owners have significantly increased the cost of the tram ride to $42 per adult, as I write this note in 2017, with some small discounts for children and for booking online in advance. This means that a group of five adults would have to fork over $200 just to get to the trailhead. Because of this unrealistic cost and the likelihood that it will continue to soar, I'll be rewriting all the hikes in a future revision to skip the tram ride. In the meantime, if you think the cost is too high, you can get out a map and easily see how you can access the same trails on foot from the Valley or Granite Trailheads.

RECOMMENDED ITINERARY: A 5-NIGHT TRIP STAYING AT:

First night: Marion Lake
Second night: Death Canyon Shelf
Third night: South Fork Cascade Canyon
Fourth night: North Fork Cascade Canyon
Fifth night: Holly Lake

THE HIKE

The Teton Crest is a long (at least three nights) shuttle hike with the incredible luxury of starting at 10,450 feet and ending at 6,875 feet, a net loss of 3,575 feet. That's not to say, however, that there is no climbing. Quite to the contrary, you must sweat your way up three big climbs, including the two most famous in the park—Hurricane Pass and Paintbrush Divide. And, of course, you go by three stunning high-country lakes—Marion Lake, Lake Solitude, and Holly Lake. Lastly, you get the best mountain scenery possible, including several miles in the shadow of the Grand Teton.

What more could you want? Three more things: good weather, a week off, and the advanced physical conditioning necessary to enjoy it.

There aren't many hikes that start out downhill, but if you take the tram from Teton Village, this can be one of them. As you stand at the main ski lodge in Teton Village, you have a tough choice. You can carry your backpack stuffed with 6 days of food and gas up 4,100 feet over 6.6 miles of constantly switchbacking service road or you can ride up the tram in 10 minutes without breaking a sweat. Tough decision, eh?

Obviously, most people choose the tram, which leaves every 15 minutes, 9 a.m. to 7:30 p.m. There's a fee to go up, but no fee to go down.

On this trip, especially on the first day, keep your map out. This route has an unusually high number of junctions, and without carefully following the map you could end up on the wrong trail.

From the tram, hike down a steep ridgeline to the junction with the service road and the park boundary. Go slowly and savor the incredible view of the Teton Range to the

The incredibly scenic Teton Crest Trail

north, including Grand Teton peeping over the skyline (you'll be on the other side of it 3 days later), and the valley to the south.

At the park boundary, turn right (west) and take one big switchback down the steep slope of Rendezvous Mountain into a bowl. You can see the trail heading up on the other side of the bowl. After the descent through some talus and subalpine vegetation, you move into spruce forest interspersed with large meadows. You'll stay in this type of terrain until Marion Lake, where you climb up to alpine country along the Teton Crest Trail.

In August and September, this route can be dry, as several intermittent streams dry up, so carry plenty of water. Horses are not allowed on the first 3.9 miles of this trail.

When you get to the next junction, take a left (west), then a right (north) at the next two junctions with trails to Moose Creek Pass and Game Creek, until you drop down into the North Fork of Granite Creek below Marion Lake. There you're treated to a short but steep climb up to the lake.

Marion Lake is a little jewel tucked in the shadow of mighty Housetop Mountain and surrounded by wildflower-carpeted meadows, and it is a great choice for the first night out.

When you leave Marion Lake in the morning, you face a 0.4-mile climb up to the park boundary and an unnamed divide on the flanks of Housetop Mountain. Then, to Fox Creek Pass it's mostly level, alpine hiking with spectacular views all around, especially of aptly named Spearhead Mountain off to the right (east).

Just before reaching Fox Creek Pass, you come to a confusing junction (no sign when we were there) with a trail going off to the left (west) down Fox Creek into the Jedediah Smith Wilderness. Turn right (north). Just over a small hill you'll see Fox Creek Pass and the park boundary. At the pass, you can either go right (northeast) down Death Canyon or left (north); you want to go left and continue along the Teton Crest Trail on Death Canyon Shelf.

The next 11 miles—over Fox Creek Pass, along Death Canyon Shelf, up and down Mount Meek Divide, through Alaska Basin, and up Hurricane Pass—are the absolute essence of the Teton Range, the choicest of the choice for mountain scenery. I've been backpacking for more than 40 years; this is definitely a truly memorable stretch of trail. I'm sure you'll agree.

The Death Canyon Shelf is a flat bench on the east flanks of a series of awesome peaks—Fossil Mountain, Bannon Peak, Mount Jedediah Smith, and Mount Meek. To the east, you can look down Death Canyon all the way to Jackson Hole. The shelf is a great choice for the second night out. It's exposed to weather, though, so be prepared, and water can be hard to find in September.

From Mount Meek Divide, you drop down into gorgeous Alaska Basin. Several small lakes dot the basin, along with a labyrinth of trails. All are distinct and well signed, however, so you should not have a problem finding your way past Basin Lakes and Sunset Lake and up to Hurricane Pass. And indeed, a hurricane-force wind almost blew us off the pass when we were there, so no problem figuring out how the name came to be.

From the pass you can see it all, including Grand Teton (and Middle and South Teton), Mount Moran to the north, and, right below you, Schoolroom Glacier. Unless the weather prohibits a long stay (as it did when I was there), spend some quality time on Hurricane Pass identifying all the peaks.

The trip from Marion Lake to Hurricane Pass might have been the best ever, but the section between the pass and Holly Lake rivals it for scenic beauty. The trail down Hurricane Pass is steep at the top but soon becomes a nicely switchbacked trail. If you have some extra time, set up camp near the top of the South Fork Cascade Camping Zone and take a side trip up toward Avalanche Divide for a close-up view of the three Tetons.

After a night along the South Fork of Cascade Creek, drop down to the junction with the main trail up Cascade Canyon. You could bail out at this point and go down to the west-shore boat dock on Jenny Lake, but if you do, you'll miss Lake Solitude and the Paintbrush Divide, so go left (northwest) at this junction.

The trail up the North Fork of Cascade Creek is forested at first but soon breaks out into subalpine meadows and a virtual kaleidoscope of wildflowers. It's 2.7 miles to Lake Solitude, but you probably want to set up your fourth camp somewhere near the top of the North Fork Cascade Camping Zone. It will only be a short walk up to Lake Solitude after camp has been set up. Lake Solitude is remote but sometimes not as quiet as it used to be. It's now a popular destination, so don't expect to have it to yourself.

After the fourth night below Lake Solitude, psych yourself up for the biggest hill of the trip, the 2.4 miles up to 10,700-foot Paintbrush Divide. The trail is in great shape, and when you stop to rest you have some great scenery to enjoy—Lake Solitude and Mica Lake below and Grand Teton to the southeast.

Paintbrush Divide might not be quite as awesome as Hurricane Pass, but it's a very close second. After soaking up the scenery for a while, start down the divide into Paintbrush Canyon on one big switchback through a talus slope and, even in September, over some snowbanks clinging to this north-facing slope. In fact, it's often dangerous to try this slope without an ice axe until August. Before you leave on this trip, be sure to quiz a ranger on the snow conditions on Paintbrush Divide. If an ice axe is recommended, be sure you know how to use it to rescue yourself if you fall. If this is beyond your capabilities, delay this trip until snow conditions improve.

If you're doing a 5-night trip, plan on Holly Lake for your last night in paradise. The junction is only 1.3 miles from the divide, but it's another 0.3 mile uphill to the lake and about that far over to the campsites on the east end of the cirque containing Holly Lake.

After your night at Holly Lake, follow the rest of the cutoff trail left (east) from the lake. Rejoin the main trail down Paintbrush Canyon 0.4 mile from the lake and gradually drop out of the high country into the mature forest of the low country.

When you get to the junction with the String Lake Trail, go left (east) and hike a mere 0.7 mile to the bridge over the short stream between String Lake and Leigh Lake. Cross the bridge to the junction with the Leigh Lake Trail just on the other side of the bridge, turn right (south), and hike a super-flat 0.8 mile along String Lake back to the

Leigh Lake Trailhead and String Lake Picnic Area parking lot, where you're likely to feel somewhat disappointed to be ending a truly remarkable backpacking trip.

Camping: For the first night out, you have four choices. Marion Lake has three heavily used campsites and a good water source, nice views (although you can only see the lake from the first campsite and then just barely), and two raised tent pads each. Marion Lake may be the best choice for the first night out because it's nicely located at 6.6 miles from the tram.

Although not as convenient, you can also camp at the Middle Fork Camping Zone or the Upper Granite Canyon Camping Zone. Upper Granite has nicer campsites along the stream with good water sources. The Middle Fork campsites generally offer better views, but water can be scarce in many areas, especially in late August and September when intermittent streams dry up. Marion Lake has designated campsites, but the two camping zones allow you to find your own campsite. For the fourth choice, you can hike past Marion Lake and camp outside the park.

For the second night, you probably want to strive for the Death Canyon Shelf and the open camping zone with no designated campsites. Water is scarce on the south part of the shelf but adequately abundant from the midpoint on. The scenery from camp will be the best possible. There's enough room to find privacy, and rest assured that the air-conditioning will be on.

If you're trying to cover this route with 4 nights out, hike past the shelf and camp anywhere in Alaska Basin. This is outside the park, so NPS regulations don't apply. However, be sure to walk softly and set up a no-trace camp in this fragile highland.

For the next night out, you can opt for either the South Fork Cascade or North Fork Cascade Camping Zones. Both areas have indicated sites, but you can camp anywhere in these areas. The indicated sites are nicely set up, however, so we can't imagine wanting to find something new. All of these campsites (and there are plenty) are outstanding. The main issue is how far you want to go that day. The camping in the North Fork is probably even nicer than in the South Fork because most sites come with a stunning view of Grand Teton.

Holly Lake has three designated campsites about a quarter-mile from the lake at the end of a trail that crosses the outlet on rocks and goes up on a slope above the lake. Campsite 3 is the most private. Surprisingly, the campsites do not have good views right from camp. Water is fairly accessible from all three sites, which have two tent pads each and a shared food storage box.

The Lower Paintbrush Canyon Camping Zone has nine indicated campsites strategically located on high points above the trail. Most are private (about 100 yards from the trail) but have only one tent pad (the NPS plans to add more later). Some of them have a fairly long hike to water. Most of the campsites are five-star with a great view.

You can also camp in the Upper Paintbrush Camping Zone along the main trail below Holly Lake. This zone requires a camping permit different from the one for Holly Lake even though they aren't far apart.

Options: This hike can be taken in reverse, but you face more climbing because at the end you will need to get up Rendezvous Mountain on foot. You can bail out and make the trip shorter by coming down Death Canyon or Cascade Canyon.

Side trips: If you have the time and energy (and enough granola bars!), try the side trips up to Static Peak Divide and Avalanche Divide.

MILES AND DIRECTIONS

0.0	Top of the Teton Village Tram.
0.4	Junction with tram service road and park boundary, bear right.
3.9	Junction with Middle Fork Cutoff Trail, turn left.
4.4	Junction with Teton Crest Trail, turn right.
5.4	Junction with Game Creek Trail. right.
6.0	Junction with North Fork Trail, turn left.
6.6	Marion Lake.
7.0	Park boundary.
8.8	Junction with trail down Fox Creek, turn right.
8.9	Fox Creek Pass and junction with Death Canyon Trail, turn left.

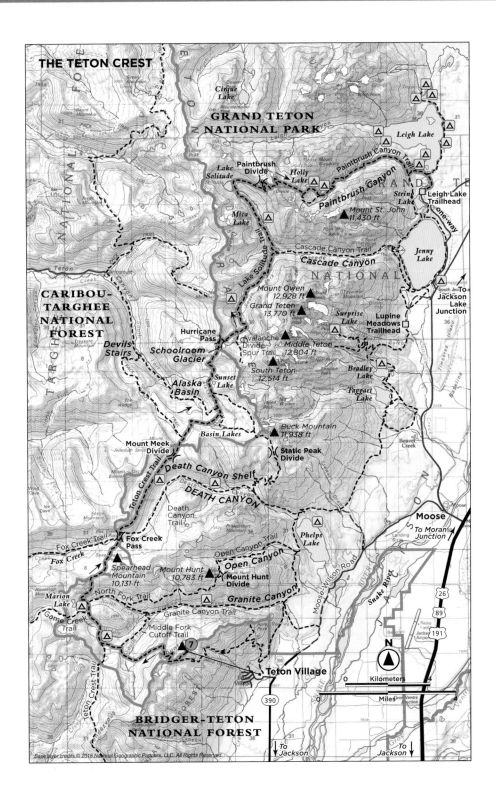

THE TETON CREST

GRAND TETON
NATIONAL PARK

Cirque
Lake

Leigh Lake

CARIBOU-
TARGHEE
NATIONAL
FOREST

Lake
Solitude

Paintbrush
Divide

Holly
Lake

Paintbrush Canyon Trail

Paintbrush Canyon

G R A N D T E T

Leigh Lake
Trailhead

String
Lake

Mica
Lake

Mount St. John
11,430 ft

one-way

Cascade Canyon Trail

Cascade Canyon

Jenny
Lake

N A T I O N A L

Mount Owen
12,928 ft

Grand Teton
13,770 ft

Surprise
Lake

South Jen To
Jackson
Lake
Junction

Hurricane
Pass

Devils
Stairs

Schoolroom
Glacier

Avalanche
Divide
Spur Trail

Middle Teton
12,804 ft

Lupine
Meadows
Trailhead

Alaska
Basin

Sunset
Lake

South Teton
12,514 ft

Bradley
Lake

Mount Meek
Divide

Basin Lakes

Buck Mountain
11,938 ft

Taggart
Lake

Static Peak
Divide

Beaver
Creek

Teton Crest Trail

Death Canyon Shelf

DEATH CANYON

Death
Canyon
Trail

Moose

To Moran
Junction

Fox Creek Trail

Fox Creek Pass

Open Canyon Trail

Phelps
Lake

Open Canyon

Fox Creek

Spearhead
Mountain
10,131 ft

Mount Hunt
10,783 ft

Mount Hunt
Divide

North Fork Trail

Granite Canyon

Marion
Lake

Game Creek
Trail

Granite Canyon Trail

26

89
191

Middle Fork
Cutoff Trail

7

Teton Village

N

Kilometers

0   4

Teton Crest Trail

BRIDGER-TETON
NATIONAL FOREST

Miles

390

To
Jackson

To
Jackson

Snake River

Moose-Wilson Road

The mighty Grand Teton, looming over most of the park
CASEY SCHNEIDER

12.4	Mount Meek Divide and park boundary.
12.6	Junction with trail to Devils Stairs, turn right.
14.4	Basin Lakes.
14.6	Junction with trail to Buck Mountain Pass, turn left.
15.4	Junction with second trail to Buck Mountain Pass, turn left.
15.7	Sunset Lake.
17.4	Hurricane Pass and Schoolroom Glacier.
19.0	Junction with trail to Avalanche Pass, turn left.
22.5	Junction with Cascade Canyon Trail, turn left.
25.2	Lake Solitude.
27.6	Paintbrush Divide.
28.9	Junction with spur trail to Holly Lake, turn left.
29.2	Holly Lake.
29.7	Return to main trail in Paintbrush Canyon, turn left.
33.9	Junction with String Lake Trail, turn left.
34.6	Junction with Leigh Lake Trail, turn right.
35.4	Leigh Lake Trailhead and String Lake Picnic Area.

JENNY LAKE AREA

Taking home a photo memory
from Leigh Lake

8 HIDDEN FALLS

WHY GO?

A scenic boat ride combined with a short stroll to a spectacular waterfall, one of the park's most famous features.

THE RUNDOWN

Start: South Jenny Lake Visitor Center and Boat Dock
Distance: 1.2-mile out and back
Difficulty: Easy
Nat Geo TOPO! Map (USGS): Jenny Lake

Nat Geo Trails Illustrated Map: Grand Teton National Park
Other maps: Earth Walk Press Grand Teton map; NPS handout map

FINDING THE TRAILHEAD

Take US 89 north of Jackson for 11.5 miles and turn left (west) at the Moose Junction. Drive past the Moose Visitor Center and through the entrance station (about a mile after turning off the highway). Follow this paved park road for another 6.8 miles from the entrance station to the South Jenny Lake turnoff. Turn left (west) here and drive less than 0.5 mile to the South Jenny Lake Boat Dock and Visitor Center. From the north, drive 12.8 miles from the Jackson Lake Junction and turn right (west) at the South Jenny Lake turnoff. The South Jenny Lake area has a general store, visitor center, boat dock, toilet facilities, and usually plenty of room to park. This is a heavily used area, and the boat ride across the lake is very popular, so in midday during the summer, the parking lot can be full. From the South Jenny Lake Boat Dock, take the short boat ride across the lake to the west-shore boat dock. The boat leaves every 15 to 20 minutes for a small fee. No facilities at the west-shore boat dock. **GPS:** 43.751604 / -110.725388

THE HIKE

Hidden Falls is one of those must-see spots in Grand Teton, and it seems, almost everybody does see it. If you go in mid-morning or in the afternoon, the trail might seem like a crowded subway. If you go in early morning, catching the first boat at 7 a.m., though, you might have the spectacular waterfall all to yourself.

After unloading from the shuttle boat, a short trail leads up to the trail that encompasses Jenny Lake. Go straight at this junction, across that mail trail, following the signage to Hidden Lake. Just before the falls, a trail veers off to the right to Lower Inspiration Point, a nice side trip if you are interested. From this junction, it's only about 200 yards to the falls, and only a bit over a half-mile in total from the boat dock.

The NPS has excellent signage throughout the area, so no chance of getting off the correct route.

Hidden Falls on the Jenny Lake loop hike
CASEY SCHNEIDER

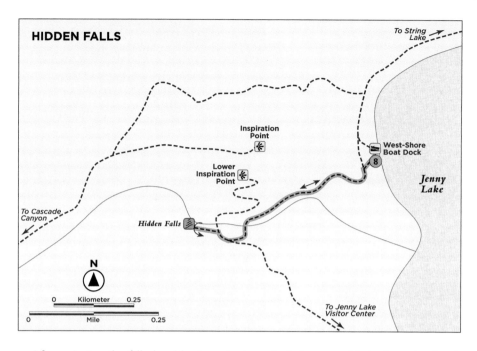

After enjoying the falls, head back to the boat dock for your ride back to the South Jenny Visitor Center.

Option: If you're feeling ambitious, you can hike the 2.3 miles back to the South Jenny Visitor Center around the south end of the lake. If interested, take a right (south) when you get back to the main lake trail instead of going straight down to the west side boat dock.

MILES AND DIRECTIONS

0.0   West-shore boat dock.

0.1   Jenny Lake Trail, go straight across trail.

0.5   Junction with trail to Lower Inspiration Point, turn left.

0.6   Hidden Falls.

1.2   West-shore boat dock.

9 INSPIRATION POINT

WHY GO?

A short uphill day hike to a prominent viewpoint overlooking Jenny Lake.

THE RUNDOWN

Start: South Jenny Lake Visitor Center and Boat Dock
Distance: 3.6-mile out and back
Difficulty: Easy
Nat Geo TOPO! Map (USGS): Jenny Lake

Nat Geo Trails Illustrated Map: Grand Teton National Park
Other maps: Earth Walk Press Grand Teton map; NPS handout map

FINDING THE TRAILHEAD

Take US 89 north of Jackson for 11.5 miles and turn left (west) at the Moose Junction. Drive past the Moose Visitor Center and through the entrance station (about a mile after turning off the highway). Follow this paved park road for another 6.8 miles from the entrance station to the South Jenny Lake turnoff. Turn left (west) here and drive less than 0.5 mile to the South Jenny Lake Boat Dock and Visitor Center. From the north, drive 12.8 miles from the Jackson Lake Junction and turn right (west) at the South Jenny Lake turnoff. The South Jenny Lake area has a general store, visitor center, boat dock, toilet facilities, and usually plenty of room to park. This is a heavily used area, and the boat ride across the lake is very popular, so in midday during the summer, the parking lot can be full. From the South Jenny Lake Boat Dock, take the short boat ride across the lake to the west-shore boat dock. The boat leaves every 15 to 20 minutes for a small fee. No facilities at the west-shore boat dock. **GPS:** 43.751604 / -110.725388

THE HIKE

The Inspiration Point Trail is not quite as crowded as the hike to Hidden Falls, but close to it. Again, the best time to see it without rubbing elbows with a lot of other hikers is early in the morning.

When you get to the west side boat dock, go up to the main trail that encompasses Jenny Lake, only a few steps from the boat dock, and turn right (north). Go about a half-mile to the main trail up Cascade Canyon (still called Horse Bypass Trail on some old maps).

Turn left (west) here and climb a steep mile-long, switchbacked hill to the junction with the Inspiration Point trail where you go left (east) and hike another 0.3 mile to Inspiration Point.

Jenny Lake from Inspiration Point
NATIONAL PARK SERVICE

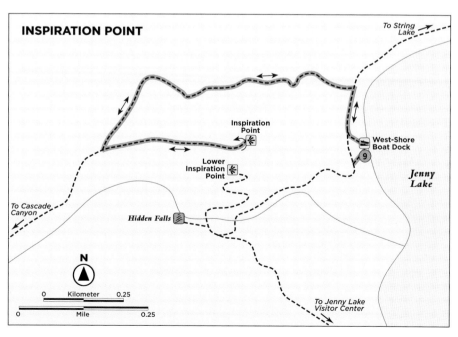

INSPIRATION POINT

To String Lake

Inspiration Point

Lower Inspiration Point

West-Shore Boat Dock

9

Jenny Lake

To Cascade Canyon

Hidden Falls

To Jenny Lake Visitor Center

N

Kilometer 0.25

Mile 0.25

Taking in the view at Inspiration Point

You used to be able to do a little loop by hiking from Hidden Falls directly over to Inspiration Point, but the NPS has closed this trail for reclamation work, and it will remain closed for several years while the area recovers from overuse.

And yes, you can get inspired from Inspiration Point where you can soak in a wonderful panoramic view of Jenny Lake and the mountains to the east.

MILES AND DIRECTIONS

0.0   West-shore boat dock.

0.1   Jenny Lake Trail, turn right.

0.5   Horse Bypass Trail, turn left.

1.5   Inspiration Point spur trail, turn left.

1.8   Inspiration Point.

3.6   West-shore boat dock.

10 **LEIGH LAKE**

WHY GO?

A really flat, really scenic day hike or easy overnighter along the shoreline of two lakes.

FINDING THE TRAILHEAD

Take US 89 north of Jackson for 11.5 miles and turn left (west) at the Moose Junction. Drive past the Moose Visitor Center and through the entrance station (about a mile after turning off the highway). Follow this paved park road for another 9.7 miles from the entrance station to the Jenny Lake turnoff. Turn left (west) here and drive 0.6 mile (follow the signs and take two right turns) to the String Lake Trailhead and 0.3 mile farther, the String Lake Picnic Area. From the north, drive 9.9 miles from the Jackson Lake Junction and turn right (west) at the Jenny Lake turnoff. Park in the large parking lot at the picnic area, which has toilet facilities. The Leigh Lake Trailhead is in the northwest corner of the picnic area. **GPS:** 43.789162 / -110.731655

THE HIKE

Although Leigh Lake is a nice hike in July, August, and September, it's also a good choice for May or June. The snow leaves this area much sooner than the high country. The scenery is unbeatable with Mount Moran and Rockchuck Peak looming above Leigh Lake and the narrow Paintbrush and Leigh Canyons slicing into the Teton Range above the west shore on each side of Mount Woodring, the high peak between Moran and Rockchuck.

The trail is in terrific shape (often double wide), and sandy beaches provide inviting rest spots along both String Lake and Leigh Lake. In addition to being one of the best day hikes in the park, Leigh Lake also provides a wonderful choice for an easy overnighter, ideal for the beginning backpacker or a family with children wanting to experience that first night in the wilderness.

Halfway along String Lake, a horse trail comes in from the right (east). From this point on, don't be surprised to see a string of horses with park visitors getting their first horse-riding experience. At the end of String Lake, go right (north) at the junction, onto the

Valley Trail. At this point you see a portage trail for people hauling their canoes up to Leigh Lake. The foot trail angles off to the right of the portage trail.

After a short, 0.2-mile walk through lodgepole pines, you get your first view of enormous Leigh Lake, a 250-foot-deep lake formed by the glaciers that once flowed out of Leigh and Paintbrush Canyons. The trail closely follows the shoreline, with Mount Moran providing the scenic backdrop. About halfway along Leigh Lake, you pass by the east-shore campsites, complete with sandy beaches and world-class vistas. The end of the lake is about 0.4 mile past the campsites. You can turn around at the campsites or the end of the lake about a half-mile more down the trail.

Camping: The campsites on the east shore of Leigh Lake are extraordinarily nice. You get a spectacular view of Mount Moran and the Teton Range right from the food areas. Each campsite has a fire pit, two or three good tent sites, and a metal bear box for storing food and garbage. Since the three campsites are on the lakeshore, water is readily accessible. The first of the three is a group site. The only knock on these sites is that the trail goes right by them, sacrificing privacy, but they would all still be rated five-star by most people camping there. Campsite GPS: Campsite 12A, 43.813 / -110.718; Campsite 12B, 43.815 / 110.718; and Campsite 12C, 43.816 / -110.728

Option: If you don't want to retrace your steps all the way back, you can turn right (west) at the junction at the end of String Lake and take the String Lake Trail back to the picnic area. This adds 2.5 miles to your hike. Refer to the description of String Lake.

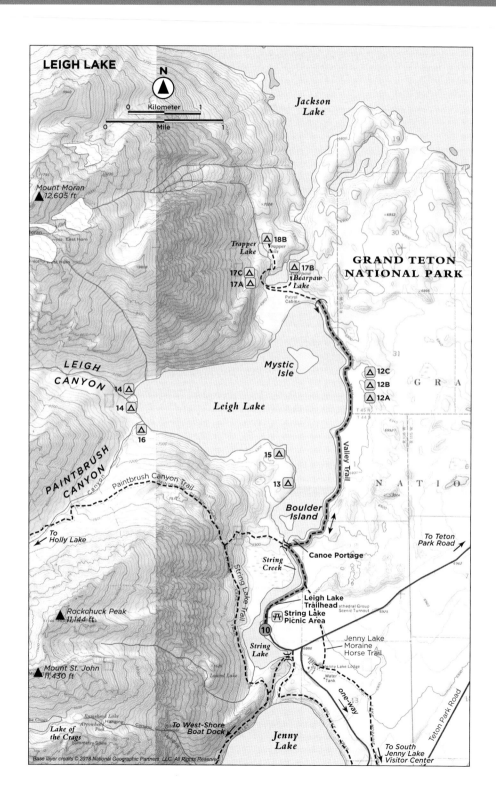

LEIGH LAKE

N

0   Kilometer   1

0   Mile   1

Jackson Lake

Mount Moran
12,605 ft

Trapper Lake

18B
Trapper Lake

17C   17B
17A   Bearpaw Lake

Patrol Cabin

GRAND TETON
NATIONAL PARK

Mystic Isle

LEIGH CANYON

14

14

16

Leigh Lake

12C
12B
12A

Valley Trail

15

13

PAINTBRUSH CANYON

Paintbrush Canyon Trail

To Holly Lake

Boulder Island

NATIO

To Teton Park Road

String Creek

Canoe Portage

String Lake Trail

Leigh Lake Trailhead
String Lake Picnic Area

Cathedral Group Scenic Turnout

Rockchuck Peak
11,144 ft

10

Jenny Lake Moraine Horse Trail

Jenny Lake Lodge

Mount St. John
11,430 ft

String Lake

Laurel Lake

Water Tank

one-way

Lake of the Crags

To West-Shore Boat Dock

Jenny Lake

Teton Park Road

To South Jenny Lake Visitor Center

Side trips: If you need more hiking, you can hike up to Bearpaw Lake, which adds 2.4 miles to the total distance. Add another 0.8 mile by continuing up to Trapper Lake.

MILES AND DIRECTIONS

0.0	Leigh Lake Trailhead at String Lake Picnic Area.
0.4	Horse trail comes in from the east.
0.8	End of String Lake and junction with trail to Holly Lake; turn right onto Valley Trail.
1.0	Leigh Lake.
2.4	East-shore campsites.
2.8	End of Leigh Lake; turn around.
5.6	Leigh Lake Trailhead at String Lake Picnic Area.

Leigh Lake
CASEY SCHNEIDER

11 STRING LAKE

WHY GO?
A short hike around a small, placid lake.

THE RUNDOWN
Start: String Lake Trailhead
Distance: 3.4-mile loop
Difficulty: Easy
Nat Geo TOPO! Map (USGS): Jenny Lake

Nat Geo Trails Illustrated Map:
Grand Teton National Park
Other maps: Earth Walk Press Grand Teton map; NPS handout map

FINDING THE TRAILHEAD
Take US 89 north of Jackson for 11.5 miles and turn left (west) at the Moose Junction. Drive past the Moose Visitor Center and through the entrance station (about a mile after turning off the highway). Follow this paved park road for another 9.7 miles from the entrance station to the Jenny Lake turnoff. Turn left (west) here and drive 0.6 mile (follow the signs and take two right turns) to the String Lake Trailhead. From the north, drive 9.9 miles from the Jackson Lake Junction and turn right (west) at the Jenny Lake turnoff. Park in one of the large parking lots at the trailhead or picnic area. No toilets right at the trailhead, but you can find one in the nearby picnic area. **GPS:** 43.784082 / -110.727354

THE HIKE
Short hikes really don't get much nicer than this one, a mostly flat loop around a gorgeous mountain lake in the shadow of the high peaks. It's also a good choice for an early-season hike because the snow usually leaves the area long before it gives up the high country.

The first 0.3 mile of the String Lake Trail is wheelchair accessible, with magnificent views of the Teton Range over placid String Lake. This is a piedmont lake formed by

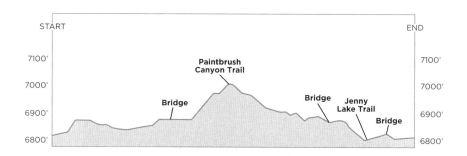

valley glaciers at the head of Paintbrush Canyon. The same goes for Jenny Lake at the head of Cascade Canyon and Leigh Lake at the head of Leigh Canyon.

After passing by the picnic area and parking lot, the trail is no longer wheelchair accessible but is still double wide and in terrific shape, with more sandy beaches and outstanding views. The Jenny Lake Moraine horse trail comes in from the east.

At the end of String Lake, go left (west) at the junction. You immediately reach a long footbridge over the short but scenic stream connecting String Lake and Leigh Lake.

From the bridge, walk through a mature forest up to the junction with the Paintbrush Canyon Trail. Go left (south) and continue through mostly open terrain down to the west shoreline of String Lake. The views aren't quite as nice here with no Teton Range backdrop, but they are still well worth the walk. At the next junction, go left (east), cross the stream between String Lake and Jenny Lake on another big footbridge, and you're back at the trailhead.

Camping: No camping allowed on this route.

Option: This loop hike can be taken in reverse with no extra difficulty.

Side trips: If you need more hiking, you can hike down to the head of Jenny Lake (0.4-mile round-trip) or up to the foot of Leigh Lake (0.3-mile round-trip).

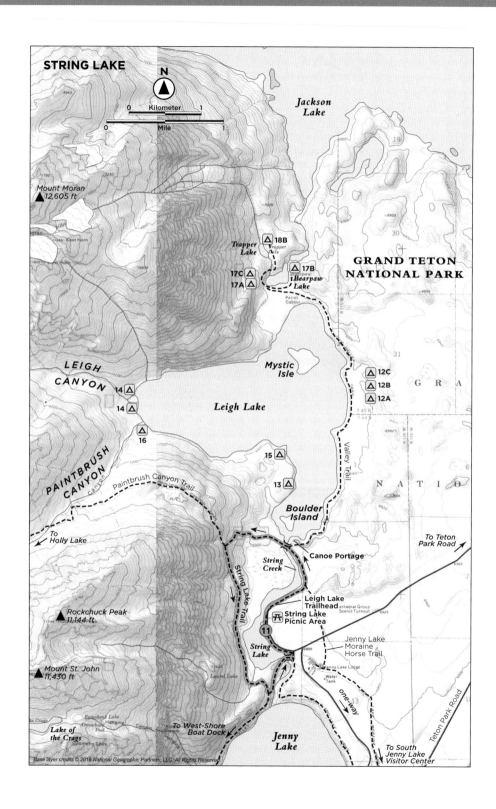

STRING LAKE

N

Kilometer
0   1

Mile
0   1

Jackson
Lake

Mount Moran
▲ 12,605 ft

Trapper
Lake   △ 18B

GRAND TETON
NATIONAL PARK

17C △   △ 17B
17A △   Bearpaw
               Lake

LEIGH
CANYON   Mystic
                          Isle

14 △

14 △   △ 12C
                    △ 12B
△   △ 12A
16

PAINTBRUSH
CANYON   Leigh Lake

         Paintbrush Canyon Trail

△ 15

To
Holly Lake   △ 13

                    Boulder
                    Island

                    Canoe Portage

                    String
                    Creek

                    Leigh Lake
                    Trailhead
         Rockchuck Peak   String Lake
         11,144 ft   Picnic Area

                    11   Jenny Lake
                               Moraine
                    String   Horse Trail
                    Lake
Mount St. John
11,430 ft   one-way

                    To West-Shore
Lake of   Boat Dock
the Crags   Jenny   To South
                               Lake   Jenny Lake
                                              Visitor Center

To Teton
Park Road

Super-scenic String Lake is accessible to any hiker.

MILES AND DIRECTIONS

0.0	String Lake Trailhead.
0.3	String Lake Picnic Area.
0.7	Horse trail comes in from the east.
1.1	End of String Lake and junction with loop trail; turn left.
1.2	Bridge over String Creek.
1.8	Junction with Paintbrush Canyon Trail; turn left.
3.1	Junction with Jenny Lake Trail; turn left.
3.3	Bridge over stream between String Lake and Jenny Lake.
3.4	String Lake Trailhead.

12 MOOSE PONDS

WHY GO?
A short loop hike for wildlife watchers.

THE RUNDOWN

Start: South Jenny Lake Visitor Center and Boat Dock
Distance: 2.6-mile lollipop loop
Difficulty: Easy
Nat Geo TOPO! Map (USGS): Jenny Lake

Nat Geo Trails Illustrated Map: Grand Teton National Park
Other maps: Earth Walk Press Grand Teton map; NPS handout map

FINDING THE TRAILHEAD

Take US 89 north of Jackson for 11.5 miles and turn left (west) at the Moose Junction. Drive past the Moose Visitor Center and through the entrance station (about a mile after turning off the highway). Follow this paved park road for another 6.8 miles from the entrance station to the South Jenny Lake turnoff. Turn left (west) here and drive less than 0.5 mile to the South Jenny Lake Visitor Center. From the north, drive 12.8 miles from the Jackson Lake Junction and turn right (west) at the South Jenny Lake turnoff. The South Jenny Lake area has a general store, visitor center, boat dock, toilet facilities, and usually plenty of room to park. This is a heavily used area, and the boat ride across the lake is very popular, so in midday during the summer, the parking lot is often full. **GPS:** 43.751604 / -110.725388

THE HIKE

The area around South Jenny Lake is heavily developed—and a bit confusing to the first-time visitor. Fortunately, if necessary, you can get your questions answered at the visitor center.

From the visitor center, start following the trail around the south edge of Jenny Lake. You immediately cross over Cottonwood Creek (outlet to Jenny Lake), along the north edge of a road, and pass the boat-launching area before getting to what looks like a real trail (Jenny Lake Trail). Follow this trail for less than a half-mile to the junction with the Moose Ponds Trail, which is on top of a glacial moraine at the south end of Jenny Lake. Go right (west) here and drop down a short but steep slope to the Moose Ponds. The trail winds through willow flats and over footbridges around the three ponds. Watch for elk and moose on the slopes above and waterfowl on the ponds.

After leaving the Moose Ponds, go through a short section of mature forest and then out into the sagebrush flats of Lupine Meadows. The last mile of the hike can also be confusing as you cross the unpaved road to the Lupine Meadows Trailhead twice and go behind the Exum Climbing School before getting back to the South Jenny Lake area.

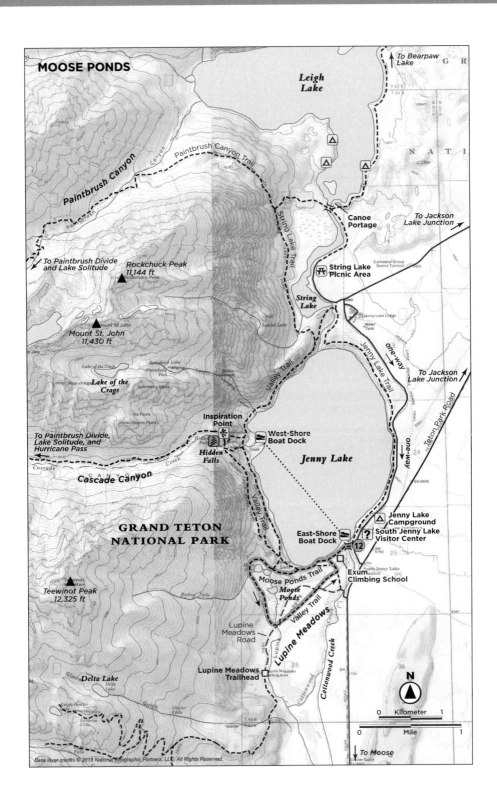

Cottonwood Creek leaving
Jenny Lake
NATIONAL PARK SERVICE

Camping: No camping allowed on this route.

Options: This loop hike can be taken in reverse with no extra difficulty. You can also add this loop to the Jenny Lake hike.

MILES AND DIRECTIONS

0.0	South Jenny Lake Visitor Center and Boat Dock.
0.1	Footbridge over Cottonwood Creek, the outlet to Jenny Lake.
0.3	Boat-launching area; junction with Jenny Lake Trail.
0.6	Junction with Moose Ponds Trail; turn right.
2.0	Lupine Meadows Road.
2.3	Lupine Meadows Road.
2.5	Exum Climbing School.
2.6	South Jenny Lake Visitor Center and Boat Dock.

13 TAGGART LAKE

WHY GO?

A short hike to a low-elevation lake.

THE RUNDOWN

Start: Taggart Lake Trailhead
Distance: 4.0-mile lollipop loop
Difficulty: Easy
Nat Geo TOPO! Map (USGS): Moose

Nat Geo Trails Illustrated Map:
Grand Teton National Park
Other maps: Earth Walk Press
Grand Teton map; NPS trail guide to
Taggart and Bradley Lakes

FINDING THE TRAILHEAD

Take US 89 north of Jackson for 11.5 miles and turn left (west) at the Moose Junction. Drive past the Moose Visitor Center and through the entrance station (about a mile after turning off the highway). Follow this paved park road for another 2.2 miles from the entrance station and turn left (west) into the Taggart Lake Trailhead. If you're coming from the north, drive 17.4 miles from the Jackson Lake Junction and turn right (west) into the trailhead parking lot. This trailhead has toilet facilities and plenty of parking. **GPS:** 43.693164 / -110.732919

THE HIKE

The short lollipop hike to Taggart Lake is one of the most accessible and popular day hikes in the park. The trail is in great shape all the way, with a few rocky sections.

The first 0.2 mile of the Taggart Lake Trail to the first junction is double wide and flat and goes through a sagebrush–dotted meadow. At the junction, go right (northwest); the trail becomes singletrack and goes past some minor development and over Taggart Creek, which you cross on a sturdy footbridge. After the creek the trail climbs gradually up to the top of a moraine, where you get consistently good views of the Teton Range, including Grand Teton. This section of the trail also goes through the track of a 1996 forest fire, so you can observe how the forest regenerates.

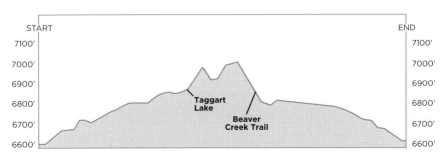

Taggart Lake
NATIONAL PARK SERVICE

When you reach the junction with the Bradley Lake Trail, go left (west) and continue for another 0.5 mile to the lake and the junction with the Valley Trail. Go left (south) here and hike along the lakeshore to a large footbridge over the outlet.

Forest-lined Taggart Lake sits at only 6,902 feet at the foot of Avalanche Canyon. You get a gorgeous view of the Grand Teton over the lake on the horizon. You can look around and see how glaciers left a moraine, which formed a natural dam to create the lake.

After leaving the lake, you hike on the Valley Trail for 0.8 mile to the junction with the Beaver Creek Trail. Go left (east) and follow Beaver Creek until you climb over a small hill (bigger in the counterclockwise direction) and drop down to the sagebrush flat to the junction with the loop trail and back to the trailhead.

Camping: No camping allowed on this route.

Option: You can take the loop in the reverse direction.

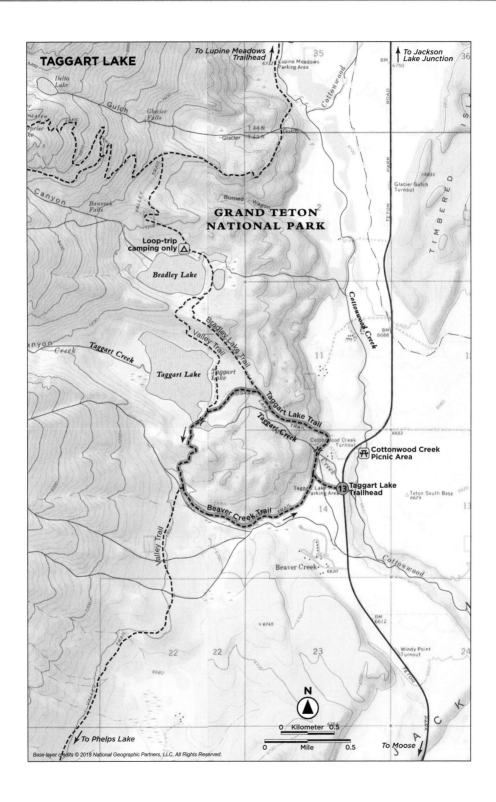

TAGGART LAKE

Delta Lake

Glacier Falls

Gulch

Glacier

Gulch

Burned Wagon

GRAND TETON
NATIONAL PARK

Bannock Falls

Canyon

Loop-trip
camping only

Bradley Lake

Bradley Lake Trail

Valley Trail

Canyon

Creek

Taggart Creek

Taggart Lake

Taggart Lake

Taggart Lake Trail

Taggart Creek

Cottonwood Creek
Turnout

Cottonwood Creek
Picnic Area

Taggart Lake
Parking Area

Taggart Lake
Trailhead

Teton South Base
6629

Beaver Creek Trail

Valley Trail

Beaver Creek

To Lupine Meadows
Trailhead

Lupine Meadows
Parking Area

To Jackson
Lake Junction

BM
6750

Glacier Gulch
Turnout

Cottonwood Creek

BM
6688

6653

Windy Point
Turnout

BM
6612

To Phelps Lake

N

0   Kilometer   0.5

0   Mile   0.5

To Moose

The famous Cathedral Group
NATIONAL PARK SERVICE

MILES AND DIRECTIONS

0.0   Taggart Lake Trailhead.

0.2   Start of loop trail; turn right.

0.4   Taggart Creek.

1.1   Junction with Bradley Lake Trail; turn left.

1.6   Taggart Lake and junction with Valley Trail; turn left.

2.4   Junction with Beaver Creek Trail; turn left.

3.8   End of loop; turn right.

4.0   Taggart Lake Trailhead.

14 BRADLEY LAKE

WHY GO?
A short hike to a low-elevation lake.

THE RUNDOWN

Start: Taggart Lake Trailhead
Distance: 4.9-mile lollipop loop
Difficulty: Easy
Nat Geo TOPO! Map (USGS): Moose

Nat Geo Trails Illustrated Map: Grand Teton National Park
Other maps: Earth Walk Press Grand Teton map; NPS trail guide to Taggart and Bradley Lakes

FINDING THE TRAILHEAD
Take US 89 north of Jackson for 11.5 miles and turn left (west) at the Moose Junction. Drive past the Moose Visitor Center and through the entrance station (about a mile after turning off the highway). Follow this paved park road for another 2.2 miles from the entrance station and turn left (west) into the Taggart Lake Trailhead. If you're coming from the north, drive 17.4 miles from the Jackson Lake Junction and turn right (west) into the trailhead parking lot. This trailhead has toilet facilities and plenty of parking. **GPS:** 43.693164 / -110.732919

THE HIKE
Bradley Lake, like Taggart Lake, was named for a member of the 1872 Hayden Expedition and, like Taggart Lake, is one of the most accessible and popular short day hikes in the park.

The first 0.2 mile of the Taggart Lake Trail to the first junction is double wide and flat and goes through a sagebrush-dotted meadow. At the junction, go right (north); the trail becomes singletrack and goes past some minor development and on to Taggart Creek, which you cross on a sturdy footbridge. After the creek the trail climbs gradually up to the top of a moraine, where you get consistently good views of the Teton Range,

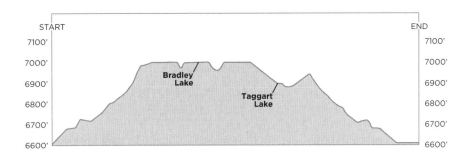

Hard to beat the view from Bradley Lake
NATIONAL PARK SERVICE

including Grand Teton. This section of the trail also goes through a 1996 forest-fire burn, so you can observe how the forest regenerates itself.

You see the Bradley Lake Trail 1.1 miles from the trailhead. Turn right (north) here and continue through 0.9 mile of the same terrain to 7,022-foot Bradley Lake, a deep

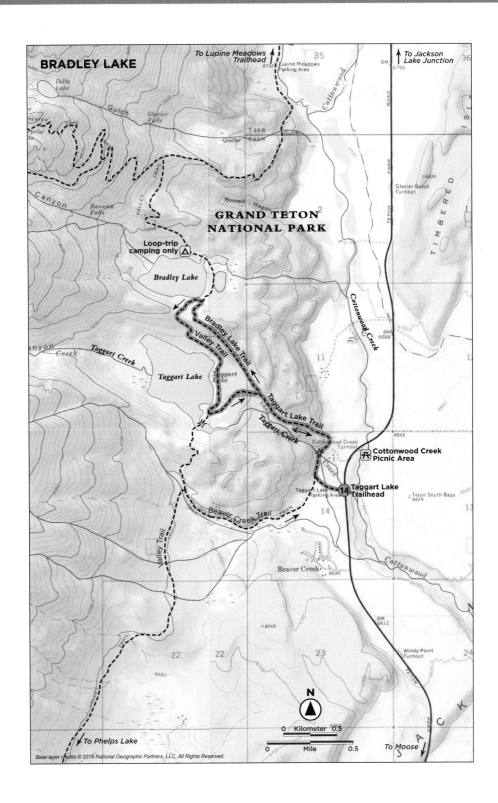

BRADLEY LAKE

To Lupine Meadows Trailhead

Lupine Meadows Parking Area

To Jackson Lake Junction

Delta Lake

Gulch

Glacier Falls

Glacier

Gulch

Burned Wagon

Bannock Falls

GRAND TETON
NATIONAL PARK

Loop-trip camping only

Bradley Lake

Bradley Lake Trail

Valley Trail

Taggart Creek

Taggart Lake

Taggart Lake

Taggart Lake Trail

Taggart Creek

Glacier Gulch Turnout

Cottonwood Creek

Cottonwood Creek Turnout

Cottonwood Creek Picnic Area

Taggart Lake Parking Area

14 Taggart Lake Trailhead

Teton South Base

Beaver Creek Trail

Valley Trail

Beaver Creek

Windy Point Turnout

To Phelps Lake

N

0 Kilometer 0.5

0 Mile 0.5

To Moose

pool at the foot of Garnet Canyon, impounded there long ago when the glacier flowing out of the canyon melted. At this point you can retrace your steps to the trailhead, but you can also add about a mile to make a loop and see two lakes instead of one. If you prefer the loop option, take a left (south) on the Valley Trail connecting Bradley and Taggart Lakes and climb over a short but steep ridge (actually another moraine) between the lakes.

It's only 1.3 miles to forest-lined Taggart Lake, which is at a slightly lower elevation (6,902 feet) but otherwise similar to Bradley Lake. I liked the view from Taggart better than from Bradley, but they are both beautiful mountain lakes.

Before you reach the footbridge over the outlet of Taggart Lake, turn left (east) on the Taggart Lake Trail and follow it for 0.5 mile back to the junction with the Bradley Lake Trail. From here, retrace your steps back to the trailhead.

Camping: Bradley Lake has one designated campsite, but it's reserved for backpackers taking the Grand Teton Loop and not available for overnighters.

Options: You can take the loop in reverse with no increase in difficulty. You can also take the out-and-back option, or you can add another 0.5 mile to the hike by following the Valley Trail south past Taggart Lake to the junction with the Beaver Creek Trail. Turn left (east) here and follow the trail back to the Taggart Lake Trailhead.

MILES AND DIRECTIONS

0.0	Taggart Lake Trailhead.
0.2	Start of loop trail; turn right.
0.4	Taggart Creek.
1.1	Junction with Bradley Lake Trail; turn right.
2.0	Bradley Lake and junction with Valley Trail; turn left.
3.3	Taggart Lake and junction with Taggart Lake Trail; turn left.
3.8	Junction with Bradley Lake Trail; turn right.
4.7	Junction with loop trail; turn left.
4.9	Taggart Lake Trailhead.

15 GARNET CANYON

WHY GO?
A popular route for those climbing the big peaks, but also a nice day hike.

THE RUNDOWN

Start: Lupine Meadows Trailhead
Distance: 8.2-mile out and back
Difficulty: Moderate
Nat Geo TOPO! Map (USGS): Moose

Nat Geo Trails Illustrated Map: Grand Teton National Park
Other maps: Earth Walk Press Grand Teton map; NPS handout map

FINDING THE TRAILHEAD
Take US 89 north of Jackson for 11.5 miles and turn left (west) at the Moose Junction. Drive past the Moose Visitor Center and through the entrance station (about a mile after turning off the highway). Follow this paved park road for another 6.6 miles from the entrance station and turn left (west) onto a gravel road at the Lupine Meadows turnoff. Follow this road for 1.4 miles until it ends at the trailhead parking lot. From the north, drive 21.8 miles from the Jackson Lake Junction and turn right (west) at the Lupine Meadows turnoff. The trailhead has toilet facilities and a huge parking area, but this trailhead is so popular that it can be full, especially at midday. You can find a general store at the South Jenny Lake turnoff about a mile to the north. **GPS:** 43.734525 / -110.741637

THE HIKE
Garnet Canyon is a main artery to several popular climbing routes in the park. Expect to see lots of people on the trail and a large parking lot full of vehicles at the trailhead. Still, it's a nice day hike with limited hill climbing.

From Lupine Meadows, the first 0.5 mile of the trail goes through mature forest with nice views of Grand Teton to the right. It then climbs up a ridge to the junction with the Garnet Canyon Trail, which also goes to Surprise and Amphitheater Lakes. Turn right

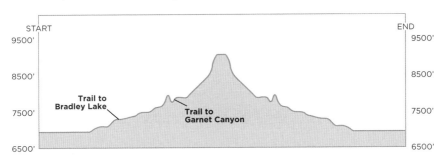

Yellow columbines

(west) and start a series of switchbacks up to another junction with the Garnet Canyon Trail. Go left (south) here and hike on a gradually ascending trail above the stream to where it ends in a large boulder field.

You get a nice view of Middle Teton much of the way up the canyon. You can actually hike farther up the canyon, and many climbers do. In fact, you'll probably see groups of climbers scrambling out through the boulders. From this point on, however, it is off-trail hiking. After a rest, retrace your steps to the Lupine Meadows Trailhead.

Camping: The NPS allows camping in the off-trail upper reaches of the canyon. If interested, inquire about camping at the Moose Visitor Center or the Jenny Lake Ranger Station.

Side trips: You can take the side trip up to Surprise and Amphitheater Lakes, which adds 3.6 miles to the distance of your trip.

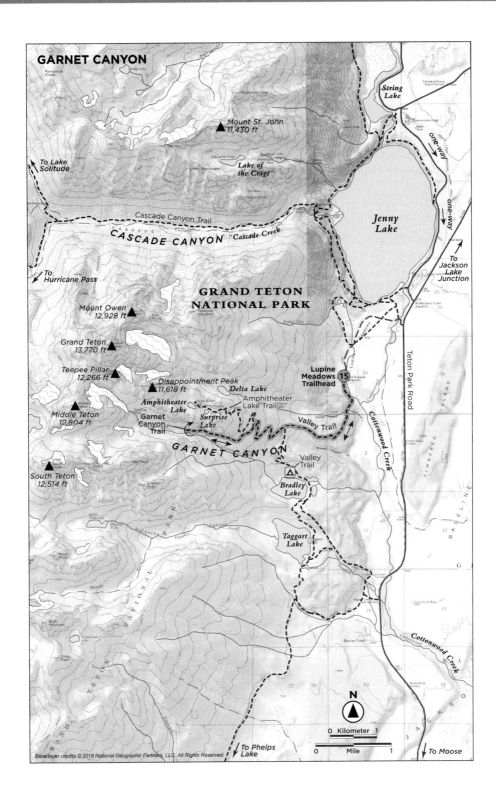

GARNET CANYON

Mount St. John
11,430 ft

To Lake
Solitude

Lake of
the Crags

String
Lake

Cascade Canyon Trail

CASCADE CANYON   Cascade Creek

Jenny
Lake

To
Hurricane Pass

GRAND TETON
NATIONAL PARK

To
Jackson
Lake
Junction

Mount Owen
12,928 ft

Grand Teton
13,770 ft

Teepee Pillar
12,266 ft

Disappointment Peak
11,618 ft

Delta Lake

Amphitheater
Lake

Amphitheater
Lake Trail

Lupine
Meadows
Trailhead   15

Middle Teton
12,804 ft

Garnet
Canyon
Trail

Surprise
Lake

Valley Trail

Teton Park Road

GARNET CANYON

South Teton
12,514 ft

Valley
Trail

Bradley
Lake

Cottonwood Creek

Taggart
Lake

To Phelps
Lake

N

0   Kilometer   1

0   Mile   1

To Moose

Hiking down the North Fork
Cascade Creek after cresting
the Paintbrush Divide
CASEY SCHNEIDER

MILES AND DIRECTIONS

0.0   Lupine Meadows Trailhead.

1.7   Junction with trail to Bradley Lake; turn right.

3.0   Junction with trail to Garnet Canyon; turn left.

4.1   End of maintained trail; turn around and retrace your steps to the trailhead.

8.2   Lupine Meadows Trailhead.

16 BEARPAW AND TRAPPER LAKES

WHY GO?
A fairly long, but flat route to four mountain lakes.

THE RUNDOWN

Start: Leigh Lake Trailhead
Distance: 8.8-mile out and back
Difficulty: Moderate
Nat Geo TOPO! Map (USGS): Jenny Lake

Nat Geo Trails Illustrated Map: Grand Teton National Park
Other maps: Earth Walk Press Grand Teton map; NPS handout map

FINDING THE TRAILHEAD

Take US 89 north of Jackson for 11.5 miles and turn left (west) at the Moose Junction. Drive past the Moose Visitor Center and through the entrance station (about a mile after turning off the highway). Follow this paved park road for another 9.7 miles from the entrance station to the Jenny Lake turnoff. Turn left (west) here and drive 0.6 mile (follow the signs and take two right turns) to the String Lake Trailhead and 0.3 mile farther, the String Lake Picnic Area. If you're coming from the north, drive 9.9 miles from the Jackson Lake Junction and turn right (west) at the Jenny Lake turnoff. Park in the large parking lot at the picnic area, which has toilet facilities. The Leigh Lake Trailhead is in the northwest corner of the picnic area. **GPS:** 43.789162 / -110.731655

THE HIKE

If you like to hike to lakes, this is the best hike in the park. It's very rare to be able to visit four low-elevation lakes (without roads to them!) on one moderate hike without climbing any big hills. This scenic and flat route makes a pleasant day hike or overnighter with a variety of great campsites.

Although this is a nice hike in July, August, and September, it's also a good choice for May or June. The snow leaves this area much sooner than the high country. The scenery is unbeatable with Mount Moran and Rockchuck Peak looming above Leigh Lake and the narrow Paintbrush and Leigh Canyons slicing into the Teton Range above the west shore on each side of Mount Woodring, the high peak between Moran and Rockchuck.

The trail is in terrific shape (often double wide), and sandy beaches provide inviting rest spots along both String Lake and Leigh Lake. In addition to being one of the best day hikes in the park, Leigh Lake also provides a wonderful choice for an easy overnighter, ideal for the beginning backpacker or a family with children wanting to experience that first night in the wilderness.

Taking a break on the shore of Trapper Lake

Halfway along String Lake, a horse trail comes in from the right (east). From this point on, don't be surprised to see a string of horses with park visitors getting their first horse-riding experience. At the end of String Lake, go right (north) at the junction, onto the Valley Trail. At this point you see a portage trail for people hauling their canoes up to Leigh Lake. The foot trail angles off to the right of the portage trail.

After a short, 0.2-mile walk through lodgepole pines, you get your first view of enormous Leigh Lake, a 250-foot-deep lake formed by the glaciers that once flowed out of Leigh and Paintbrush Canyons. The trail closely follows the shoreline, with Mount Moran providing the scenic backdrop. About halfway along Leigh Lake, you pass by the east-shore campsites, complete with sandy beaches and world-class vistas. The end of the Leight Lake is about a half-mile trail.

When you leave Leigh Lake, you pass through a forested area, part of which is recovering nicely from a 1981 forest fire. Just before you reach Bearpaw Lake, you enter a large meadow. The junction for the loop around the lake is in the middle of this meadow. You can obviously take the loop either way around the lake, but this description follows the clockwise route, so bear left (northwest) at this junction.

As you near the lake, the trail drops down into the trees surrounding the shore and follows the shoreline to campsites 17A and 17C. The trails around these two campsites can get confusing, so be alert. The trail to Trapper Lake stays low and goes over a makeshift footbridge over the inlet to Bearpaw Lake and then up on a small ridge where it turns north and heads for Trapper Lake.

After 0.4 mile of walking a level, forest-lined trail, you reach Trapper Lake. It has a nice bench with an overlook of Trapper Lake, a great place for a relaxing lunch to the music of trout jumping in the lake. Campsite 18B is slightly farther up the trail toward the inlet of the lake.

From here, retrace your steps to Bearpaw Lake. You can go back around the west side of the lake, but you can also take a social trail over to campsite 17B on the northeast shore of the lake, where there is an official trail back to the junction south of the lake. The social trail requires a little agility, as you have to cross over the shallow outlet of Bearpaw Lake on logs and rocks.

From the junction, retrace your steps back to the String Lake Picnic Area.

Camping: The campsites on the east shore of Leigh Lake are extraordinarily nice. You get a spectacular view of Mount Moran and the Teton Range right from the food areas. Each campsite has a fire pit, two or three good tent sites, and a metal bear box for storing food and garbage. Since the three campsites are on the lakeshore, water is readily accessible. The first of the three is a group site. The only knock on these sites is that the trail goes right by them, sacrificing privacy, but they would all still be rated five-star by most people camping there. Campsite GPS: Campsite 12A, 43.813 / -110.718; Campsite 12B, 43.815 / 110.718; and Campsite 12C, 43.816 / -110.728

Bearpaw Lake has three campsites. Three-star 17A is on the west shore near the lake but has a marginal view of it. It has two tent sites, a fire pit, and good access to water, but the trail goes right by the campsite. Four-star 17C is up the hill from 17A and is more private with a slightly better view. It also has a fire pit and good access to water from the inlet to the lake. These two campsites share the same bear box and bear pole. Five-star 17B is on the northeast shore of the lake by the outlet. It has a terrific view of the lake and the Teton Range in the background, good access to water, a fire pit, and a bear box, and is reasonably private. GPS: Campsite 17A, 43.831 / -110.732; Campsite 17B, -43.832 / -110.728; and Campsite 17C, 43.830 / -110.732

Trapper Lake has one campsite. Five-star 18B is near the outlet, has a fire pit and a nicer view, and is close to water. GPS: Campsite 18B, 43.834 / -110.731

Option: If you don't want to retrace your steps all the way, you can turn right (west) at the junction at the end of String Lake and take the String Lake Loop Trail back to the picnic area. This adds 2.5 miles to your hike.

MILES AND DIRECTIONS

0.0   Leigh Lake Trailhead.

0.4   Horse trail comes in from the east.

0.8   End of String Lake and junction with trail to Holly Lake; turn right.

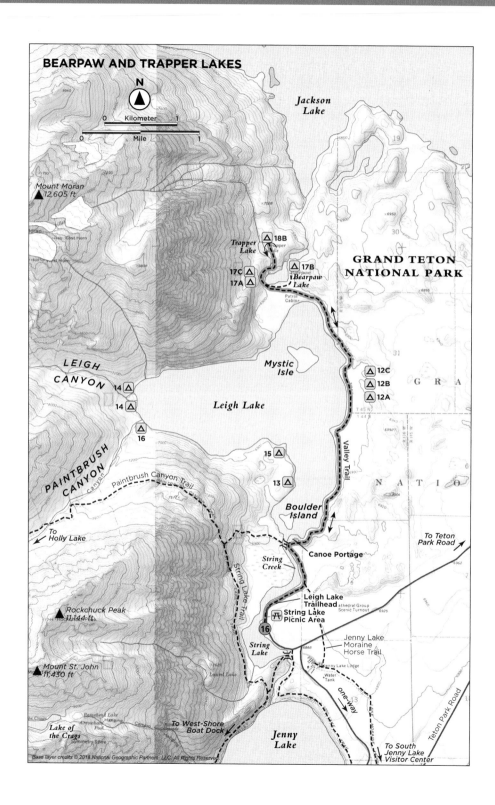

BEARPAW AND TRAPPER LAKES

N

Kilometer

Mile

Jackson Lake

▲ Mount Moran
12,605 ft

East Horn

GRAND TETON
NATIONAL PARK

Trapper Lake
18B
17C 17B
17A Bearpaw Lake

Patrol Cabin

LEIGH CANYON

Mystic Isle

14
14
16

Leigh Lake

12C
12B
12A

GRA

15

NATIO

PAINTBRUSH CANYON

Paintbrush Canyon Trail

13

Boulder Island

Valley Trail

To Holly Lake

String Creek

Canoe Portage

To Teton Park Road

String Lake Trail

Rockchuck Peak
11,144 ft

Leigh Lake Trailhead
String Lake Picnic Area

Cathedral Group Scenic Turnout

16

Jenny Lake Moraine Horse Trail

▲ Mount St. John
11,430 ft

String Lake

Laurel Lake

Jenny Lake Lodge

Water Tank

one-way

To West-Shore Boat Dock

Lake of the Crags

Jenny Lake

To South Jenny Lake Visitor Center

Teton Park Road

1.0   Leigh Lake.

2.4   East-shore campsites.

2.7   End of Leigh Lake.

3.3   Junction with loop trail around Bearpaw Lake.

4.0   North end of Bearpaw Lake.

4.4   Trapper Lake; retrace your steps back to the trailhead.

8.8   Leigh Lake Trailhead.

17 SURPRISE AND AMPHITHEATER LAKES

WHY GO?

A popular day hike or overnighter to two high-country lakes in the shadow of the Grand Teton.

THE RUNDOWN

Start: Lupine Meadows Trailhead
Distance: 9.6-mile out and back
Difficulty: Moderate
Nat Geo TOPO! Map (USGS): Moose

Nat Geo Trails Illustrated Map: Grand Teton National Park
Other maps: Earth Walk Press Grand Teton map; NPS handout map

FINDING THE TRAILHEAD

Take US 89 north of Jackson for 11.5 miles and turn left (west) at the Moose Junction. Drive past the Moose Visitor Center and through the entrance station (about a mile after turning off the highway). Follow this paved park road for another 6.6 miles from the entrance station and turn left (west) onto a gravel road at the Lupine Meadows turnoff. Follow this road for 1.4 miles until it ends at the trailhead parking lot. From the north, drive 21.8 miles from the Jackson Lake Junction and turn right (west) at the Lupine Meadows turnoff. The trailhead has toilet facilities and a huge parking area, but this trailhead is so popular that it can be full, especially at midday. You can find a general store at the South Jenny Lake turnoff about a mile to the north. **GPS:** 43.734525 / -110.741637

THE HIKE

This is one of the most popular hikes in the park, so expect to see lots of people on the trail and a large parking lot full of vehicles at the trailhead.

From Lupine Meadows, the first 0.5 mile of the Valley Trail goes through mature forest with nice views of Grand Teton off to the right. It then climbs up a ridge to the junction

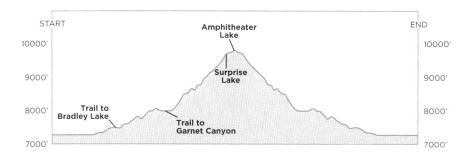

Glacier lilies carpet the high country.

with the trail to Garnet Canyon, which also goes to Surprise and Amphitheater Lakes. Turn right (west) here and start a series of switchbacks up to the lakes. At several points you get sweeping views of Bradley and Taggart Lakes to the southeast and Jenny Lake to the northeast, as well as the rest of the valley floor.

At the 3-mile mark, turn right (west) again at the junction with the Garnet Canyon Trail. When you get to Surprise Lake, the only surprise will be how beautiful it is, with Teepee Pillar, Disappointment Peak, Mount Owen, and much more of the Teton Range, including Grand Teton, majestically looming in the background over the lake.

Amphitheater Lake, only 0.2 mile up the trail, is at least as nice, with an amphitheater view of the high peaks. After enjoying these two gems of the Teton Range, retrace your steps to the Lupine Meadows Trailhead.

Camping: Surprise Lake has three campsites on a ridge on the east side of the lake with a mostly obstructed view of the lake and the high peaks, and a moderate walk to water.

Side trip: You can take a side trip up to the end of Garnet Canyon, which adds 2.2 miles to the distance of your trip.

MILES AND DIRECTIONS

0.0   Lupine Meadows Trailhead.

1.7   Junction with trail to Bradley Lake; turn right.

3.0   Junction with trail to Garnet Canyon; turn right.

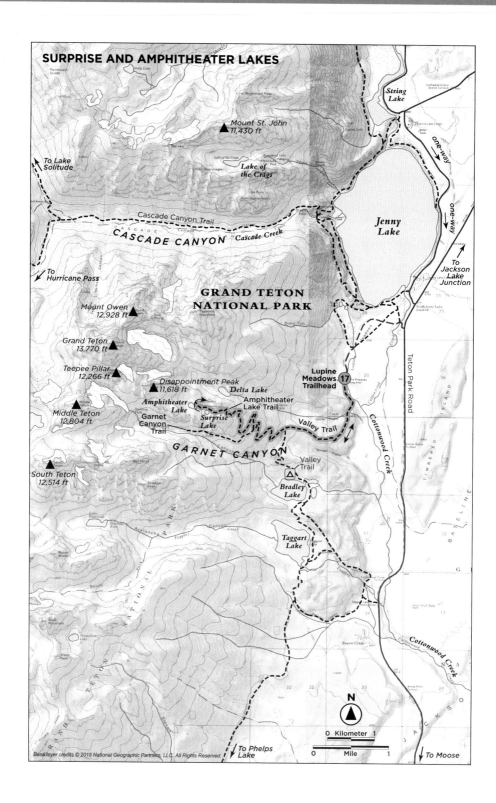

SURPRISE AND AMPHITHEATER LAKES

Surprise Lake
NATIONAL PARK SERVICE

18 JENNY LAKE

WHY GO?

A loop hike around the shoreline of a centerpiece of Grand Teton National Park.

THE RUNDOWN

Start: String Lake Trailhead
Distance: 7.7-mile loop
Difficulty: Moderate
Nat Geo TOPO! Map (USGS): Jenny Lake

Nat Geo Trails Illustrated Map: Grand Teton National Park
Other maps: Earth Walk Press Grand Teton map; NPS handout map

FINDING THE TRAILHEAD

Take US 89 north of Jackson for 11.5 miles and turn left (west) at the Moose Junction. Drive past the Moose Visitor Center and through the entrance station (about a mile after turning off the highway). Follow this paved park road for another 9.7 miles from the entrance station to the Jenny Lake turnoff. Turn left (west) here and drive 0.6 mile (follow the signs and take two right turns) to the String Lake Trailhead and Picnic Area. If you're coming from the north, drive 9.9 miles from the Jackson Lake Junction and turn right (west) at the Jenny Lake turnoff. If you plan to start at South Jenny Lake, go to the South Jenny Lake turnoff, which is 2.9 miles south of the Jenny Lake turnoff on the main park road. Park in one of the large parking lots at the trailhead or the picnic area. There are no toilet facilities right at the trailhead, but you can find them at the nearby picnic area. The South Jenny Lake area has a general store, visitor center, boat dock, toilet facilities, and plenty of room to park. **GPS:** 43.784082 / -110.727354

THE HIKE

There aren't many hikes of this distance that follow the shoreline of a beautiful lake most of the way. This makes the Jenny Lake loop hike one of the most popular in the park.

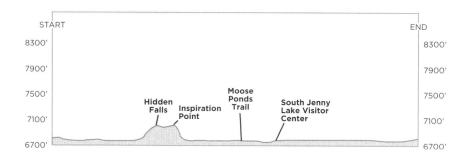

Jenny Lake from the east shore trail
NATIONAL PARK SERVICE

You can start at either South Jenny Lake or the String Lake Trailhead at the north end of Jenny Lake. This trail description follows the counterclockwise route starting from the String Lake Trailhead. This allows you to hike the more remote west side of the lake in the morning hours, stop for a snack at the South Jenny Lake general store, visit a visitor center without driving to it, and enjoy a scenic walk along the more developed, but more scenic, east shore after lunch.

The trail starts about 100 yards south of the trailhead parking lot at the bridge over the stream leaving String Lake. Go right (west) here and cross the bridge. In 0.2 mile you turn left (south) onto the Valley Trail at the junction with the String Lake Trail.

After this junction, hike along the stream between String Lake and Jenny Lake for about a quarter-mile until you get your first view of Jenny Lake at the inlet. From here the trail follows the lakeshore until you get near the boat dock area on the west side of the lake. You might not see many hikers on the trail to the boat dock, but expect to see lots of people in the dock area because the boat ride across Jenny Lake is very popular. Many park visitors take the boat over to see Hidden Falls and Inspiration Point.

As you approach the boat dock area, the trail veers away from the lake slightly. At this point, you can take a short spur trail down to see the dock and the lake and the 0.8-mile round-trip up to see Hidden Falls and to marvel at the view from Inspiration Point.

After being inspired on Inspiration Point, go back to the main trail and continue along the lake to the South Jenny Lake area. The west-side trail gets rocky in a few places but

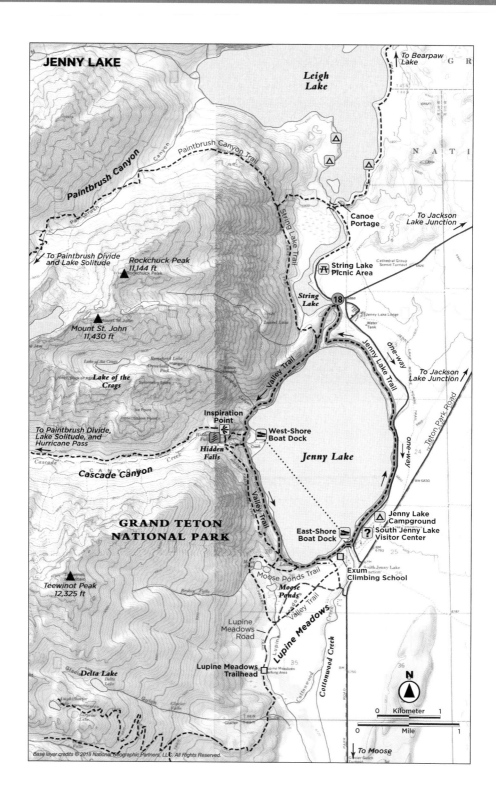

JENNY LAKE

Leigh Lake

To Bearpaw Lake

G R

N A T I

Paintbrush Canyon

Paintbrush Canyon Trail

Canoe Portage

To Jackson Lake Junction

To Paintbrush Divide and Lake Solitude

Rockchuck Peak 11,144 ft

String Lake Trail

String Lake Picnic Area

Cathedral Group Scenic Turnout

String Lake

18

Jenny Lake Lodge

Water Tank

Mount St. John 11,430 ft

Lake of the Crags

Valley Trail

Jenny Lake Trail

one-way

To Jackson Lake Junction

Teton Park Road

Inspiration Point

West-Shore Boat Dock

To Paintbrush Divide, Lake Solitude, and Hurricane Pass

Hidden Falls

Cascade Canyon

Jenny Lake

one-way

24

BN G830

GRAND TETON NATIONAL PARK

East-Shore Boat Dock

Jenny Lake Campground

South Jenny Lake Visitor Center

Teewinot Peak 12,325 ft

Moose Ponds Trail

Moose Ponds

Exum Climbing School

South Jenny Lake Junction

25

Valley Trail

26

Lupine Meadows Road

Lupine Meadows

Valley Trail

Lupine Meadows

Cottonwood Creek

Delta Lake

Lupine Meadows Trailhead

Lupine Meadows Parking Area

35

36

N

0   Kilometer   1

0   Mile   1

To Moose

is mostly flat and uncrowded. The trail closely follows the lakeshore after the boat dock area, but gradually pulls away from the lake as you reach the junction with the Moose Ponds Trail. Go left (south) at this junction. The developed southern section of Jenny Lake can get confusing, but stay on the trail near the lake, and you eventually come to the visitor center area. You pass by the Jenny Lake boat launch, a vehicle campground, other buildings and developments, and then over a long footbridge over the outlet of Jenny Lake and on to the visitor center area. This is slightly more than halfway through the hike, so it's a good time to lie back, get a snack at the general store, and check out the interpretive displays in the visitor center before continuing up the east shore of the lake.

The trail through the developed area is paved, but the pavement ends about a quarter-mile up the lakeshore. The trail on the east shore is more heavily used and in better shape than on the west shore, and the one-way scenic drive parallels the trail for part of the way. Most hikers would agree that the scenery is also better on the east shore, where you can enjoy classic views of the high peaks across the lake.

Camping: No camping allowed on this route.

Options: This loop hike can be taken in either direction. You can also make this a 4.6-mile shuttle and skip the developed east side of the lake by leaving a vehicle at one end and hiking only the more remote west side of the lake to see Hidden Falls.

Side trips: Don't miss the 0.4-mile side trip up to Hidden Falls. Keep going up to Inspiration Point (another 0.4 mile) for a panoramic view of Jenny Lake.

MILES AND DIRECTIONS

0.0	String Lake Trailhead.
0.1	Bridge over outlet of String Lake.
0.3	Valley Trail to Jenny Lake inlet; turn left.
2.2	West-shore boat dock and spur trails to Hidden Falls/Inspiration Point.
4.0	Junction with Moose Ponds Trail; turn left.
4.3	Boat-launching area.
4.5	Bridge over outlet of Jenny Lake.
4.6	South Jenny Lake Visitor Center and Boat Dock; start of paved trail.
4.8	End of paved trail.
7.7	String Lake Trailhead.

19 HOLLY LAKE

WHY GO?

A gradual uphill day hike or overnighter to a gorgeous mountain lake in one of the famous canyons of the Teton Range.

THE RUNDOWN

Start: Leigh Lake Trailhead
Distance: 12.6-mile out and back
Difficulty: Difficult day hike; moderate overnighter
Nat Geo TOPO! Map (USGS): Jenny Lake

Nat Geo Trails Illustrated Map: Grand Teton National Park
Other maps: Earth Walk Press Grand Teton map; NPS handout map

FINDING THE TRAILHEAD

Take US 89 north of Jackson for 11.5 miles and turn left (west) at the Moose Junction. Drive past the Moose Visitor Center and through the entrance station (about a mile after turning off the highway). Follow this paved park road for another 9.7 miles from the entrance station to the Jenny Lake turnoff. Turn left (west) here and drive 0.6 mile (follow the signs and take two right turns) to the String Lake Trailhead and 0.3 mile farther, the String Lake Picnic Area. If you're coming from the north, drive 9.9 miles from the Jackson Lake Junction and turn right (west) at the Jenny Lake turnoff. Park in the large parking lot at the picnic area, which has toilet facilities. The Leigh Lake Trailhead is in the northwest corner of the picnic area. **GPS:** 43.789162 / -110.731655

THE HIKE

Starting this hike at the Leigh Lake Trailhead instead of the String Lake Trailhead gives you great scenery for the first 0.8 mile along the east shore of String Lake. In the morning hours when skies are more likely to be clear, you can soak in the spectacular views of the Teton Range across String Lake.

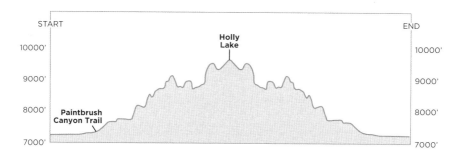

After the first 0.8 mile on a double-wide trail, take a left (west) at the junction at the north end of String Lake. The trail immediately crosses over the inlet of String Lake on a long footbridge and then goes through mature forest until you reach the Paintbrush Canyon Trail 0.7 mile later. Go right (northwest) and start a gradual ascent up Paintbrush Canyon.

As you climb, the forest thins out; the higher you go the more colorful it gets. This canyon not only has lots of Indian paintbrush but also many other species of wildflowers. Take a moment here and there to look back for a nice view of Leigh Lake and Jackson Lake.

When you reach the junction with the Holly Lake Trail, go right (north) for a fairly steep 0.5-mile climb to the little jewel of a lake in the shadow of Mount Woodring. I saw a huge black bear grazing on the slope above the lake while having lunch there.

After a good rest or overnight stay at the lake, retrace your steps back to the Paintbrush Canyon Trail and proceed to the junction with the String Lake Trail. From this junction, retrace your steps to the trailhead.

Camping: The Lower Paintbrush Canyon Camping Zone has nine indicated campsites strategically located on high points above the trail. Most of them are private (about 100 yards from the trail) but have only one tent pad (the Park Service plans to add more later). Some of them require a fairly long hike to water. Most are excellent campsites with a good view.

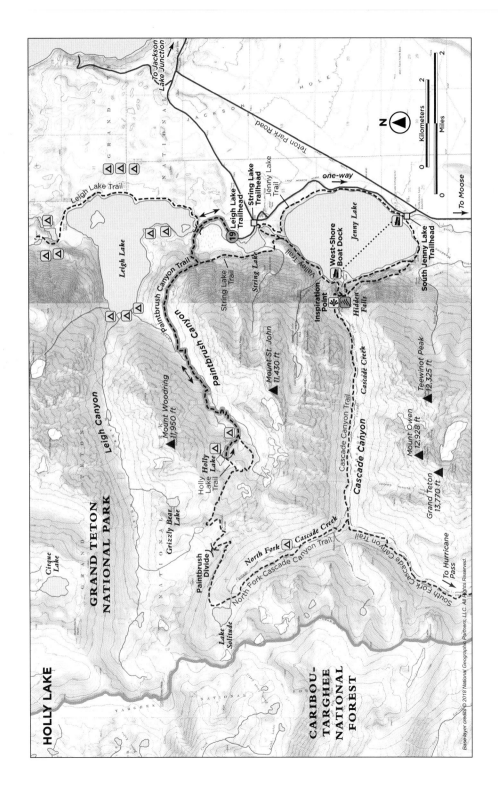

HOLLY LAKE

You can also camp at one of three other designated campsites. These campsites are about a quarter-mile from Lake Holly at the end of a trail that crosses the outlet on rocks and goes up on a slope above the lake. Campsite 3 is the most private. None of the campsites have a good view. Water is fairly accessible from all three sites, which have two tent pads each and a shared metal food storage box.

Moss campion
National Park Service

Option: From the junction with the String Lake Trail on the return trip, you can make a loop around String Lake. Go right (south) and hike about 0.5 mile through mostly open slope, down to the west shore of String Lake, where the trail stays most of the rest of the way to the junction with the Jenny Lake Trail. Go left (east) and over the outlet of String Lake 0.2 mile later. At the end of the footbridge, go left (north) and follow the paved trail back to the String Lake Picnic Area and the Leigh Lake Trailhead. This loop adds only 0.1 mile to your trip.

MILES AND DIRECTIONS

0.0   Leigh Lake Trailhead.

0.4   Horse trail comes in from the east.

0.8   End of String Lake and junction with trail to Holly Lake; turn left.

0.9   Footbridge over inlet of String Lake.

1.6   Paintbrush Canyon Trail; turn right.

5.8   Junction with Holly Lake Trail; turn right.

6.3   Holly Lake.

12.6   Leigh Lake Trailhead.

20 CASCADE CANYON

WHY GO?

A classic hike into the main canyon below Grand Teton.

THE RUNDOWN

Start: South Jenny Lake Visitor Center and Boat Dock
Distance: 8.8-mile out and back
Difficulty: Moderate
Nat Geo TOPO! Map (USGS): Jenny Lake

Nat Geo Trails Illustrated Map: Grand Teton National Park
Other maps: Earth Walk Press Grand Teton map; NPS handout map

FINDING THE TRAILHEAD

Take US 89 north of Jackson for 11.5 miles and turn left (west) at the Moose Junction. Drive past the Moose Visitor Center and through the entrance station (about a mile after turning off the highway). Follow this paved park road for another 6.8 miles from the entrance station to the South Jenny Lake turnoff. Turn left (west) here and drive less than 0.5 mile to the South Jenny Lake Visitor Center and Boat Dock. From the north, drive 12.8 miles from the Jackson Lake Junction and turn right (west) at the South Jenny Lake turnoff. From the South Jenny Lake Boat Dock, take the short boat ride across the lake to the west-shore boat dock. The boat leaves every 15 to 20 minutes for a small fee. The South Jenny Lake area has a general store, visitor center, boat dock, toilet facilities, and usually plenty of room to park. This is a heavily used area, and the boat ride across the lake is very popular, so in midday during the summer, the parking lot can be full. No facilities at the west-shore boat dock. **GPS:** 43.751604 / -110.725388

THE HIKE

The mouth of Cascade Canyon around Hidden Falls and Inspiration Point is probably the most heavily used spot in Grand Teton National Park. Thousands of park visitors take the scenic boat ride across Jenny Lake and mill around the falls and Inspiration

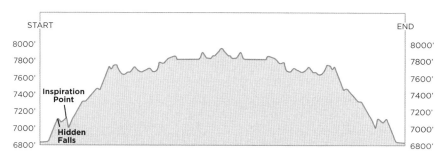

Point for a while and then return. The area shows the wear and tear of this heavy use, but there's a reason for it: The falls are spectacular, and you definitely can get inspired on Inspiration Point. Most visitors to Hidden Falls and Hidden Falls Overlook do not take the scenic hike up Cascade Canyon, so once you've gone past the Inspiration Point trail, the traffic thins out dramatically.

This route used to go to Hidden Falls, then to Inspiration Point, before heading up Cascade Canyon. However, the NPS has closed the trail between Hidden Falls for reclamation work and it will remain closed for several years, so now, you need to take what used to be called the Horse Bypass Trail. If you want to see Hidden Falls and Inspiration Point, these will be short side trips from your main route.

Sugarbowl
National Park Service

The hike up the canyon climbs seriously for about the first mile and then goes into a gradual, almost unnoticeable ascent along the cascading stream on the Cascade Canyon Trail. The steep canyon gives you one outstanding view after another all the way to the junction where the Cascade Canyon Trail splits into the South Fork to Hurricane Pass and the North Fork to Lake Solitude and the Paintbrush Divide.

After a short rest, turn around here and retrace your steps back to Jenny Lake in time to catch the boat back across the lake. If for some reason you didn't catch the boat, you can hike along the south shore of the lake 2 miles to the east-shore boat dock.

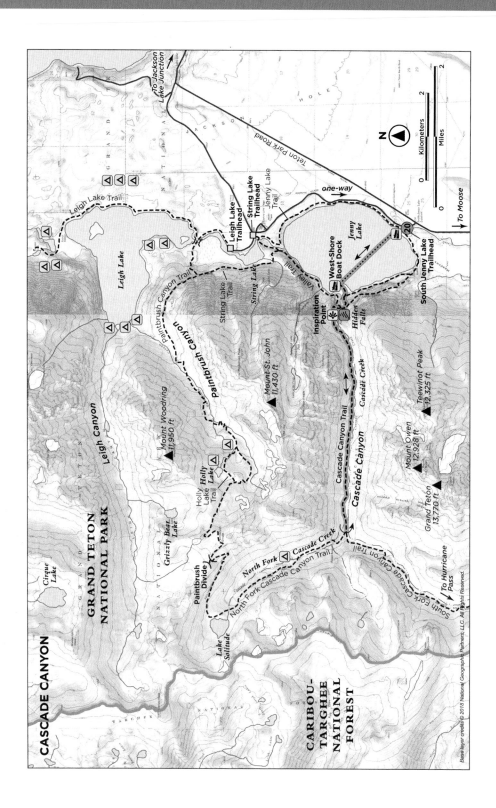

The yellow columbine
CASEY SCHNEIDER

Camping: No camping allowed on this route.

Option: If you want to leave early in the morning or don't like boats, you can hike along the south shore of Jenny Lake to get to the Hidden Falls area. This would add about 4 miles to your hike.

Side trips: Leave time to take the side trips to Hidden Falls and Inspiration Point. These short side trips are less than a mile each.

MILES AND DIRECTIONS

0.0   South Jenny Lake Visitor Center and Boat Dock.

0.1   Junction with Valley Trail; turn right (north).

0.6   Junction with Cascade Canyon Trail; turn left (west).

1.6   Junction with Inspiration Point Trail; turn right (west).

4.4   Trail forks into South and North Fork Cascade Canyon Trails; turn around and retrace your route.

8.8   South Jenny Lake Visitor Center and Boat Dock.

21 **LAKE SOLITUDE**

WHY GO?

Perhaps the most popular long hike to perhaps the most famous wilderness lake in the Teton Range.

THE RUNDOWN

Start: South Jenny Lake Visitor Center and Boat Dock
Distance: 14.2-mile out and back or shuttle
Difficulty: Difficult

Nat Geo TOPO! Map (USGS): Mount Moran
Nat Geo Trails Illustrated Map: Grand Teton National Park
Other maps: Earth Walk Press Grand Teton map; NPS handout map

FINDING THE TRAILHEAD

Take US 89 north of Jackson for 11.5 miles and turn left (west) at the Moose Junction. Drive past the Moose Visitor Center and through the entrance station (about a mile after turning off the highway). Follow this paved park road for another 6.8 miles from the entrance station to the South Jenny Lake turnoff. Turn left (west) here and drive less than 0.5 mile to the South Jenny Lake Visitor Center and Boat Dock. From the north, drive 12.8 miles from the Jackson Lake Junction and turn right (west) at the South Jenny Lake turnoff. The South Jenny Lake area has a general store, visitor center, boat dock, toilet facilities, and usually plenty of room to park. This is a heavily used area, and the boat ride across the lake is very popular, so in midday during the summer, the parking lot can be full. From the South Jenny Lake Visitor Center and Boat Dock, take the short boat ride across the lake to the west-shore boat dock. The boat leaves every 15 to 20 minutes for a small fee. No facilities at the west-shore boat dock. **GPS:** 43.751604 / -110.725388

THE HIKE

The mouth of Cascade Canyon around Hidden Falls is probably the most heavily used spot in the park. Thousands of park visitors take the scenic boat ride across Jenny Lake

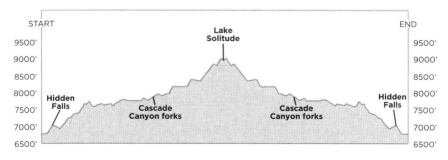

and mill around the falls and Inspiration Point for a while and then return. The area shows the wear and tear of this heavy use, but there's a reason for it: The falls are spectacular, and you can get inspired from Inspiration Point. Most visitors to Hidden Falls don't take the scenic hike up to Lake Solitude, so once you've gone past Inspiration Point, the traffic thins out dramatically.

This route used to go to Hidden Falls, then to Inspiration Point, before heading up Cascade Canyon. However, the NPS has closed the trail between Hidden Falls for reclamation work and it will remain closed for several years, so now, you need to take what used to be called the Horse Bypass Trail. If you want to see Hidden Falls and Inspiration Point, these will be short side trips from your main route.

The hike up the canyon climbs seriously for about the first mile and then goes into a gradual, almost unnoticeable ascent along the spectacular cascading stream for which the canyon was named. The steep canyon gives you one outstanding view after another all the way to the junction where the trail splits into the South Fork to Hurricane Pass and the North Fork to Lake Solitude and Paintbrush Divide.

Go right (northwest) and start the gradual 2.7-mile upgrade to 9,035-foot Lake Solitude. About halfway up, after crossing the North Fork of Cascade Creek twice on footbridges, you break out of the forest into a wildflower-carpeted cirque, which will be implanted in your memory as one of the most beautiful places you have ever been. The lake itself is at timberline, so only a few scattered trees surround it. Even in mid-August icebergs cover the lake's surface.

On most days, though, solitude can be an elusive goal at the lake. Usually, you will have to share the shoreline scenery with other hikers.

Spend as much time as you have at Lake Solitude and then start the descent back to the boat dock. For most of the 2.7 miles down to the main trail, you're staring at Grand Teton along with Mount Owen, Teewinot Peak, and other famous high points in the

September is a great month to visit Lake Solitude.
NATIONAL PARK SERVICE

Teton Range. When you reach the main Cascade Canyon Trail, go left (east) and retrace your steps to Jenny Lake. Be sure to start back in time to catch the boat across the lake. If for some reason you miss the boat, you can hike along the south shore of the lake 2 miles to the east-shore boat dock.

Camping: You can camp in the North Fork Cascade Camping Zone, which starts shortly after you turn right at the fork in the main trail and goes up to within about a half-mile of the lake. With one or two exceptions, these are memorable campsites with great views, all in the shadow of Grand Teton. You have good access to water, privacy, and two or more tent sites. Keep in mind that you can camp at any of the eleven indicated sites but aren't required to do so. You can set up a no-trace camp anywhere in the camping zone.

Option: If you want to leave early in the morning or don't like boats, you can hike along the south shore of Jenny Lake to get to the Hidden Falls area. This would add about 4 miles to your hike.

Side trip: If you have the energy and time (and make sure you have both), you can extend your trip to the top of Paintbrush Divide, another 2.4 miles above Lake Solitude. This adds 4.8 miles to the distance of this trip. Also, leave time to take the short side trips to Hidden Falls and Inspiration Point, which are less than a mile each.

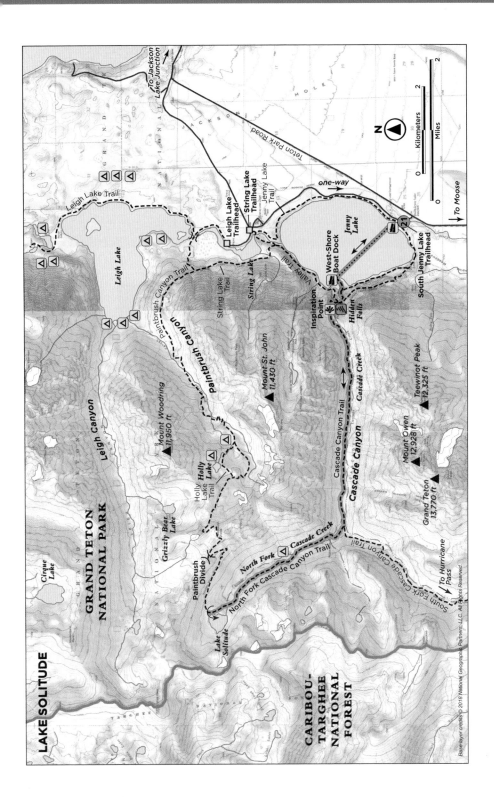

LAKE SOLITUDE

GRAND TETON NATIONAL PARK

CARIBOU-TARGHEE NATIONAL FOREST

To Jackson Lake Junction

Teton Park Road

one-way

To Moose

N

Kilometers
Miles

Leigh Lake Trail

Leigh Lake Trailhead

String Lake Trailhead

Jenny Lake Trail

Leigh Lake

String Lake Trail

Paintbrush Canyon Trail

String Lake

Valley Trail

Jenny Lake

West-Shore Boat Dock

21

South Jenny Lake Trailhead

Paintbrush Canyon

Mount St. John 11,430 ft

Inspiration Point

Hidden Falls

Cascade Creek

Teewinot Peak 12,325 ft

Leigh Canyon

Mount Woodring 11,590 ft

Cascade Canyon Trail

Cascade Canyon

Holly Lake Trail

Holly Lake

Mount Owen 12,928 ft

Grizzly Bear Lake

North Fork Cascade Creek

Grand Teton 13,770 ft

Paintbrush Divide

North Fork Cascade Canyon Trail

South Fork Cascade Canyon Trail

To Hurricane Pass

Cirque Lake

Lake Solitude

MILES AND DIRECTIONS

0.0 South Jenny Lake Visitor Center and Boat Dock.

0.1 Junction with Valley Trail; turn right (north).

0.6 Junction with Cascade Canyon Trail; turn left (west).

1.6 Junction with Inspiration Point Trail; turn right (west).

4.4 Trail forks into South and North Fork Cascade Canyon Trails; turn right (northwest).

7.1 Lake Solitude.

14.2 South Jenny Lake Visitor Center and Boat Dock.

Option: You can hike out and back from either end.

Sticky geranium
NATIONAL PARK SERVICE

22 VALLEY TRAIL

WHY GO?
A forested, low-country day hike or overnighter to three lakes.

THE RUNDOWN

Start: Lupine Meadows Trailhead
Distance: 14.9-mile shuttle
Difficulty: Difficult day hike; moderate overnighter
Nat Geo TOPO! Map (USGS): Moose

Nat Geo Trails Illustrated Map: Grand Teton National Park
Other maps: Earth Walk Press Grand Teton map; NPS handout map; NPS trail guide to Taggart and Bradley Lakes

FINDING THE TRAILHEAD

Take US 89 north of Jackson for 11.5 miles and turn left (west) at the Moose Junction. Drive past the Moose Visitor Center and through the entrance station (about a mile after turning off the highway). Follow this paved park road for another 6.6 miles from the entrance station and turn left (west) onto a gravel road at the Lupine Meadows turnoff. Follow this road for 1.4 miles until it ends at the trailhead parking lot. From the north, drive 21.8 miles from the Jackson Lake Junction and turn right (west) at the Lupine Meadows turnoff. The trailhead has toilet facilities and a huge parking area, but this trailhead is so popular that it can be full, especially at midday. You can find a general store at the South Jenny Lake turnoff about a mile to the north. **GPS:** 43.734525 / -110.741637

THE HIKE

This isn't one of the high-country adventures that most people visualize when they think of Grand Teton National Park. Instead, this is mostly a walk in the woods similar to what you would find in many western mountain ranges. The Valley Trail, which goes to three low-elevation lakes, is a popular choice for early spring because the snow gives up this low-elevation area long before the high canyons and passes.

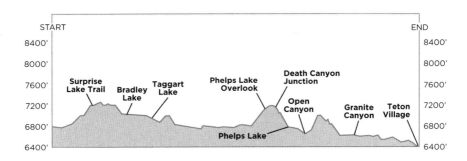

The trail is in good shape the entire way, with a hill between each lake and canyon. Some sections of the trail, mainly at the south end near Teton Village, receive heavy horse use. The trail goes through a forest mixed with lodgepole, Engelmann spruce, Douglas fir, and aspen. The southern end of the trail has more aspen and turns a wonderful aspen gold in the fall.

From Lupine Meadows, the Valley Trail starts out flat through mature forest with nice views of Grand Teton off to the right. Then it climbs up a ridge to the junction with the Surprise Lake Trail, which also goes to Garnet Canyon. Turn left (south) and drop down to Bradley Lake. After you have hiked most of the way around the small lake, you see the Bradley Lake Trail veering off to the left. Go right (south), staying on the Valley Trail, and hike over another ridge (actually a moraine) to Taggart Lake. Go right (south) at the junction with the Taggart Lake Trail and right (south) again 0.8 mile up the trail at the Beaver Creek Trail junction. Both of these trails go off to the east to the Taggart Lake Trailhead.

From the Beaver Creek Trail junction, it's 2.9 miles to the junction to the Death Canyon Trailhead. You can't actually see the trailhead when you get to the junction, but it's only 0.1 mile to the left (east), in case you need a pit toilet. Continue south by going right at this junction as the trail climbs gradually to a great overlook above Phelps Lake, a fabulous place for a little R&R. It's another 1.1 miles down to Phelps Lake (take a left at the Death Canyon Trail junction) and, if you're backpacking, your overnight campsite.

The trail skirts the west side of Phelps Lake (watch for moose; they're everywhere around Phelps Lake) and then keeps going south through the same terrain. Go left (south) at both junctions with the Open Canyon Trail less than a mile after the lake.

When you get to Granite Creek, you see the junction with the trail up Granite Canyon on the north bank of the stream. Go left (south) and cross the sturdy footbridge. Just on the other side of the stream is the junction with the trail to the Granite Canyon Trailhead, 1.6 miles to the left (east). Go right (south) and head for Teton Village. From here to the park boundary, expect to see large horse parties. Parts of this trail are heavily trampled.

After a 1.7-mile hike through aspens and small meadows, you reach the park boundary, where the horse use abruptly ends. From this point on, you go through the Teton Village Ski Area to the main lodge. The trail through the ski area can get very confusing. Follow the signs that say "Summer Hiking Trail" or "Valley Trail" to the main ski lodge. You can usually see the main lodge and tram to help stay on the right track.

Camping: Phelps Lake has three excellent campsites. As you approach the lake, watch for a junction with a trail going to the left (east) to the campsites. All three are on the lake's north shore, with a good view of the lake, fire pits, and room for two tents. Two share a food storage box; one has its own food area and bear box. The campsites are out of sight of the main trail, but they are fairly close. Please talk softly to respect the privacy of others. Bradley Lake also has a designated campsite, but this is reserved for backpackers doing the Grand Teton Loop.

Options: You can shorten this shuttle by leaving a vehicle at the Taggart Lake, Death Canyon, or Granite Canyon Trailheads.

You can take this shuttle in reverse, of course, which means you face the fairly steep climb up through the ski area. When we hiked this route, we started at Teton Village and had a frustrating experience trying to find the trail amid all the construction and roads in the first mile. Hiking from the north, it should be easier to navigate through the ski area because you can look ahead and see the main ski lodge and tram where the trail ends.

The trail goes by five spur trails back to trailheads along the eastern slope of the Teton Range, so you have lots of options for bailing out and cutting this hike short.

MILES AND DIRECTIONS

0.0   Lupine Meadows Trailhead.

1.7   Junction with Surprise Lake Trail; turn left.

3.1   Bradley Lake.

3.3   Junction with Bradley Lake Trail; turn right.

4.1   Taggart Lake.

4.2   Junction with Taggart Lake Trail; turn right.

5.0   Junction with Beaver Creek Trail; turn right.

7.9   Death Canyon Trailhead; turn right.

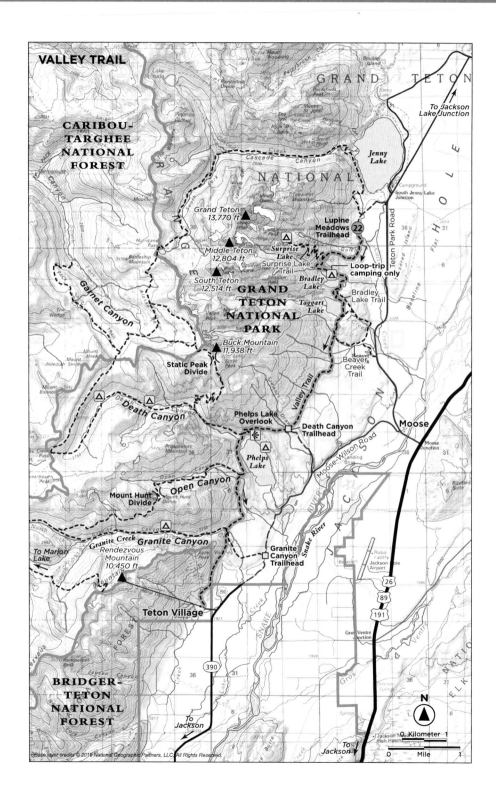

Phelps Lake
NATIONAL PARK SERVICE

8.7	Phelps Lake Overlook.
9.5	Junction with Death Canyon Trail; turn left.
9.8	Phelps Lake.
10.4	First junction with Open Canyon Trail; turn left.
10.6	Second junction with Open Canyon Trail; turn left.
12.3	Junction with Granite Canyon Trail; turn left.
12.4	Junction with trail to Granite Canyon Trailhead; turn right.
14.2	Park boundary.
14.9	Teton Village.

23 PAINTBRUSH DIVIDE

WHY GO?

One of the premier hikes in Grand Teton National Park, best as a long, hard day hike or two-day backpacking adventure.

> ### THE RUNDOWN
>
> **Start:** Leigh Lake Trailhead
> **Distance:** 19.0-mile loop
> **Difficulty:** Difficult
> **Nat Geo TOPO! Map (USGS):** Jenny Lake
>
> **Nat Geo Trails Illustrated Map:** Grand Teton National Park
> **Other maps:** Earth Walk Press Grand Teton map; NPS handout map

FINDING THE TRAILHEAD

Take US 89 north of Jackson for 11.5 miles and turn left (west) at the Moose Junction. Drive past the Moose Visitor Center and through the entrance station (about a mile after turning off the highway). Follow this paved park road for another 9.7 miles from the entrance station to the Jenny Lake turnoff. Turn left (west) here and drive 0.6 mile (follow the signs and take two right turns) to the String Lake Trailhead and 0.3 mile farther, the String Lake Picnic Area. From the north, drive 9.9 miles from the Jackson Lake Junction and turn right (west) at the Jenny Lake turnoff. Park in the large parking lot at the picnic area, which has toilet facilities. The Leigh Lake Trailhead is in the northwest corner of the picnic area. **GPS:** 43.789162 / -110.731655

THE HIKE

The famed Paintbrush Divide is a classic, long day hike for extra-fit hikers, but also works as an overnighter or 2-night backpack. It's definitely one of the premier hikes in the park, but it's best to wait until August to try it. Snow clings to the north face of Paintbrush Divide until late in the summer. Even in September you can plan on crossing a few

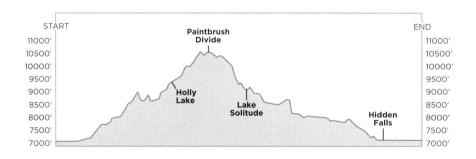

snowbanks. If you decide to go in July, check on snow conditions with rangers at the visitor center before hitting the trail.

Starting this hike at the Leigh Lake Trailhead at the String Lake Picnic Area instead of the String Lake Trailhead gives you great scenery for the first 0.8 mile along the east shore of String Lake. You can soak in the spectacular views of the Teton Range across String Lake in the morning hours when the skies are more likely to be clear. You can also start at the String Lake Trailhead and hike the west shore of String Lake in the morning, but I prefer the east-shore route.

After the first 0.8 mile on a double-wide trail, take a left (west) at the junction at the north end of String Lake. The trail immediately crosses over the inlet of String Lake on a long footbridge and then goes through mature forest until you reach the Paintbrush Canyon Trail 0.7 mile later. Go right (northwest) and start a gradual ascent up Paintbrush Canyon.

As you climb, the forest gradually thins out, and the higher you go the more colorful it gets. This canyon not only has lots of Indian paintbrush but also lots of many other wildflowers. Take a moment to look back for a nice view of Leigh Lake and Jackson Lake.

When you get to the junction with the Holly Lake Trail, you can keep going up the canyon, but I recommend going right (north) to pass by Holly Lake. After this junction, you make a fairly steep 0.5-mile climb to the little jewel of a lake in the shadow of Mount Woodring. When I did this hike, I saw a huge black bear on the slope above the lake while having lunch there.

The Paintbrush Divide's namesake
NATIONAL PARK SERVICE

After taking a break at the lake, continue for 0.4 mile and rejoin the main Paintbrush Canyon Trail. By taking the Holly Lake option, you skip 0.8 mile of main trail, which is a steeper but shorter route up Paintbrush Canyon.

Once back on the main trail, it's a 1.3-mile climb up above timberline to 10,700-foot Paintbrush Divide. The divide faces north, so plan on crossing a few snowbanks. I hiked up the divide on September 14 and still had to cross four snowbanks. The trail is well contoured to make it seem like a fairly easy ascent.

After enjoying the spectacular scenery from the divide, take an equally scenic route down to Lake Solitude. Most of the way you can see Lake Solitude and Mica Lake and Grand Teton off to the southeast. Scenery doesn't get much better than this.

Lake Solitude has become one of the most popular destinations in the park, so don't expect to have it to yourself. At 9,035 feet, the large lake sits close to timberline and is a fragile environment, so be careful not to leave your mark on what you could call "Lake Not-so-Solitude."

The scenery remains spectacular after the lake as you head down the North Fork of Cascade Creek. Grand Teton is constantly in your face, a postcard view you'd mostly miss if you did this hike clockwise. When you reach the junction with the Cascade Canyon Trail, go left (east) and head down Cascade Canyon to the boat dock. You cross the creek twice on sturdy footbridges.

Just before you get to Jenny Lake, you can take a 0.3-mile side trip over to see Inspiration Point, a beautiful overlook with a sweeping view of Jenny Lake.

This route used to go by Hidden Falls. However, the NPS has closed the trail between Hidden Falls for reclamation work, and it will remain closed for several years, so now, you need to take what used to be called the Horse Bypass Trail down to the Valley Trail along Jenny Lake. Seeing Hidden Falls and Inspiration Point now requires short side trips off the main route.

When you reach the Valley Trail along Jenny Lake, go left (north). The trail follows the shoreline of Jenny Lake for 1.5 miles to the junction with the String Lake Trail. Turn right (east) and hike another 0.3 mile to the String Lake Trailhead. From the trailhead, hike a paved trail for 0.3 mile along String Lake to the Leigh Lake Trailhead and the picnic area.

Camping: The Lower Paintbrush Canyon Camping Zone has nine indicated campsites strategically located on high points above the trail. Most of them are private (about

Wait until August to hike the Paintbrush Divide.
NATIONAL PARK SERVICE

100 yards from the trail) but have only one tent pad (the NPS plans to add more later). Some of them have a fairly long hike to water. Most of the campsites are outstanding with a good view.

Holly Lake has three designated campsites. These campsites are about a quarter-mile from the lake at the end of a trail that crosses the outlet on rocks and goes up on a slope above the lake. Campsite 3 is the most private. None of the campsites have a good view from camp. Water is fairly accessible from all three sites, which have two tent pads each and a shared food storage box.

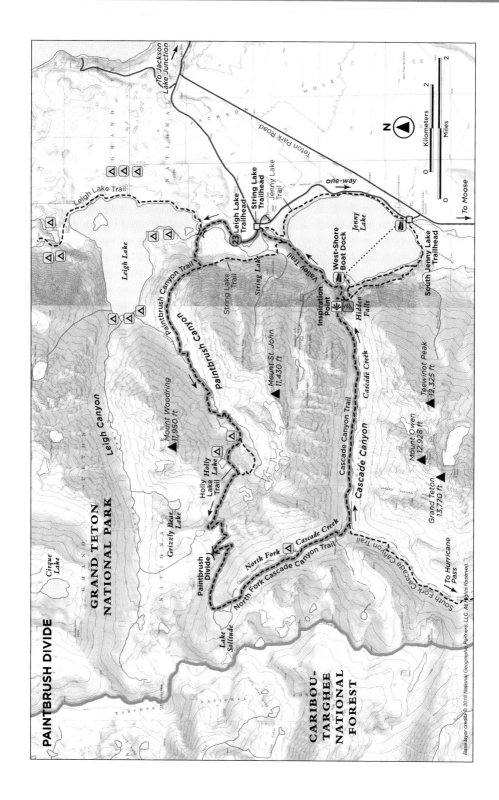

You can also camp along the main trail in the Upper Paintbrush Canyon Camping Zone about a half-mile below the lake. This is a different camping zone from Holly Lake, so make sure your permit matches your campsite.

The NPS once allowed camping at Lake Solitude, but the campsites were removed to reduce heavy use. Now you can camp just below the lake in the eleven indicated campsites in the North Fork Cascade Camping Zone. Most are five-star or four-star campsites with awesome views of Grand Teton towering over the camp and easy access to water. All campsites are well off the trail with space for at least two tents. Even though the indicated campsites are terrific, you don't have to camp there. You can set up a no-trace camp anywhere else in the North Fork Camping Zone.

Options: You can do this loop hike in reverse, but the climb up to the divide seems easier going counterclockwise as described here. Also, the scenery might be better. You can also start and finish the hike at the String Lake Trailhead or at the west-shore boat dock on Jenny Lake after taking the boat across the lake. If you've already seen Inspiration Point and Hidden Falls and are in a hurry, you can take the Horse Bypass Trail to the Jenny Lake Trail and miss this congested area, which cuts about a mile off your trip.

Side trips: If you have a lot of extra time and energy, the trail up the South Fork of Cascade Creek to Hurricane Pass would be a memorable hike, but it would add 10.2 miles to the distance of your trip. Also, be sure to leave time to see Inspiration Point and Hidden Falls, both short side trips.

MILES AND DIRECTIONS

0.0	Leigh Lake Trailhead.
0.4	Horse trail comes in from the east.
0.8	End of String Lake; turn left.
0.9	Footbridge over String Creek.
1.6	Paintbrush Canyon Trail; turn right.
5.8	Junction with Holly Lake Trail; turn right.
6.3	Holly Lake.
6.7	Return to Paintbrush Canyon Trail; turn right.
8.0	Paintbrush Divide.
10.4	Lake Solitude; junction with North Fork Cascade Canyon Trail.
13.1	Junction with Cascade Canyon Trail; turn left.
15.9	Junction with Inspiration Point Trail; turn left.
16.9	Junction with Valley Trail; turn left.
18.4	Junction with String Lake Trail; turn right.
18.7	String Lake Trailhead.
19.0	Leigh Lake Trailhead.

24 **THE GRAND TETON LOOP**

WHY GO?
An epic backpacking adventure around the heart of Grand Teton National Park.

THE RUNDOWN

Start: South Jenny Lake Visitor Center and Boat Dock
Distance: 32.2-mile loop
Difficulty: Difficult
Nat Geo TOPO! Map (USGS): Jenny Lake

Nat Geo Trails Illustrated Map: Grand Teton National Park
Other maps: Earth Walk Press Grand Teton map; NPS handout map

FINDING THE TRAILHEAD
Take US 89 north of Jackson for 11.5 miles and turn left (west) at the Moose Junction. Drive past the Moose Visitor Center and through the entrance station (about a mile after turning off the highway). Follow this paved park road for another 6.8 miles from the entrance station to the South Jenny Lake turnoff. Turn left (west) here and drive less than 0.5 mile to the South Jenny Lake Visitor Center. From the north, drive 12.8 miles from the Jackson Lake Junction and turn right (west) at the South Jenny Lake turnoff. The South Jenny Lake area has a general store, visitor center, boat dock, toilet facilities, and usually plenty of room to park. This is a heavily used area, and the boat ride across the lake is very popular, so in midday during the summer, the parking lot could be full. From the South Jenny Lake Visitor Center and Boat Dock, take the short boat ride across the lake to the west-shore boat dock. The boat leaves every 15 to 20 minutes for a small fee. If you have two vehicles, you can leave one of them at the Lupine Meadows Trailhead (about a mile walk to the south). The turnoff to Lupine Meadows is about a quarter-mile south of the South Jenny turnoff on the main park road. **GPS:** 43.751604 / -110.725388

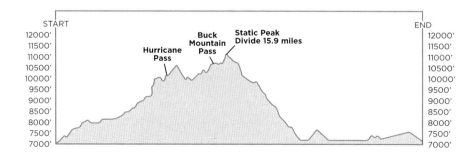

RECOMMENDED ITINERARY:
First night: Lower section of South Fork Cascade Canyon
Second night: Basin Lakes area in Alaska Basin
Third night: Phelps Lake

THE HIKE
Capturing the true essence of the Teton Range on a day hike can be challenging, but with a night or two in the shadows of the high peaks, it creeps into your insides and takes root. That's an excellent reason to take this hike.

You need at least 4 days to cover this entire loop and have any extra time for relaxing and for side trips. Even by taking 4 or 5 days, though, this is still a tough trip. Because of the position of the camping zones, you're looking at 10-plus miles on two of the days. This hike description describes a 4-day trip, but check the options section below for ways to shorten or lengthen the trip.

The trip starts with a pleasant boat ride across Jenny Lake. You can clearly see the beginning of your route, the mouth of Cascade Canyon, during the 15-minute ride. The mouth of Cascade Canyon around Hidden Falls is probably the most heavily used spot in the park. Thousands of visitors take the scenic boat ride across Jenny Lake and mill around the falls and Inspiration Point an hour or two and then return. The area shows

Hiking the Static Peak Divide on the Grand Teton Loop route
NATIONAL PARK SERVICE

Death Canyon from the
trail to Static Peak Divide
NATIONAL PARK SERVICE

the wear and tear of this heavy use and it's easy to see why. The falls are spectacular, and you really can get inspired on Inspiration Point.

Most visitors to Hidden Falls do not take the scenic hike up Cascade Canyon, so once you've gone past the spur trail to Inspiration Point, the traffic thins out dramatically. The hike up the canyon climbs seriously for about the first mile and then goes into a gradual, almost unnoticeable ascent along the, of course, cascading stream. Cascade Creek also pauses in some smooth-water sections to give a quiet contrast to the steep canyon walls on each side. Mount Owen and Teewinot Peak dominate the southern horizon. The steep canyon gives you one outstanding view after another all the way to the junction where the trail splits into the South Fork up to Hurricane Pass and the North Fork to Lake Solitude and Paintbrush Divide.

Go left (southwest). The grade becomes slightly more precipitous as you head toward Hurricane Pass. Look for a campsite in the early part of the camping zone, which starts shortly after the junction.

Start early enough the next morning to allow time for a side trip up Avalanche Divide. When you get to the junction with Avalanche Divide, hang your packs and take 2 or 3 hours enjoying a truly fantastic view of Grand Teton, Middle Teton, and South Teton, the best view of all three I found anywhere in the park. The trail to the divide is steep and gets a little hard to follow near the divide, but the incredible vistas make the pain and exhaustion go away—or at least worth it.

Back at the junction, start the climb up to Hurricane Pass—a gap in The Wall, a steep cliff along the park boundary. It's a respectable but not brutal climb to the pass. The trail is in great shape and nicely switchbacked. At this point it may give you some comfort to know that doing this hike in reverse would be even more difficult, with over 10 miles of steep upgrade in Death Canyon and up to Static Peak Divide.

On the pass, true to its namesake, it may get a bit breezy (around a Category 3 hurricane when I was there), but hang onto something long enough to get a memorable view of everything. In addition to the incredible mountain scenery, you can see gradually disappearing Schoolroom Glacier right below the pass.

From the pass, it's a short walk on the ridge before dropping down into Alaska Basin. You could call this the "no wimp zone." Anything you find up here is hardy—the alpine sunflowers, the little willows that might be 100 years old, the overstuffed marmots running around, and, of course, even the mighty backpackers who make it to Alaska Basin.

Once over the ridge and into the basin, you get a sweeping view of the entire basin and Battleship Mountain to the west. The trail goes along the west shoreline of Sunset Lake and, shortly thereafter, comes to the first of many junctions. To stay on this route, go left (east), but you may want to go over to the Basin Lakes area for your second night out. In that case, go right (south) and then left (east) at the junction just before the lakes. Both routes take you to Buck Mountain Pass and are about the same length, but the Basin Lakes route involves a slightly tougher climb.

When you get to Buck Mountain Pass, you may have the impression that it's all downhill from here. Wrong. You still have a mild climb ahead of you to get to Static Peak Divide, the third pass on this route.

The trip up Static Peak Divide and the divide itself should get your adrenaline flowing. For a short stretch you hike on a trail gouged out of a steep cliff, so be careful. If you have young children, this would be a good place to keep them on a short leash. Static Peak Divide is quite austere and ruggedly spectacular, but don't get caught in a lightning storm. Yes, that's how it earned its name.

From the divide, it's a nice high-country hike for about a mile, and then you drop into the forested south slope of Death Canyon. The trail switchbacks downward endlessly to the floor of Death Canyon, the junction with the Death Canyon Trail, and a patrol cabin.

Go left (east) and continue your downhill hike on a fairly rocky trail down Death Canyon. You can see Phelps Lake ahead, which will probably be your next campsite. If so, go right (south) at the junction above the lake. About 0.4 mile later as you approach the lake, watch for a spur trail to the left (east) going around to the campsites on the north shore of the lake.

After your stay at Phelps Lake, retrace your steps back up to the Valley Trail above the lake and take a right (north). There is a surprisingly steep hill coming out of Phelps Lake, but this is somewhat indicative of the rest of this last day. As you go from Phelps Lake

Alaska Basin-not part of the park, but it should be
NATIONAL PARK SERVICE

to Taggart Lake to Bradley Lake to the Lupine Meadows Trailhead, you climb a ridge (or a moraine in some cases) between each point—nothing very steep, but constantly up and down.

This last day, hiking along the base of the Teton Range, is quite the contrast to the first three days of the hike spent in the high country. You go through mature forest with a few aspen groves and meadows. Watch for moose, black bears, and other wildlife, especially around Phelps Lake, where I also saw a rare rubber boa on the trail.

About 2 miles after Phelps Lake, go left (north) at the junction with the trail to the Death Canyon Trailhead. Also take left turns at the Beaver Creek, Taggart Lake, and Bradley Lake junctions. Glaciers created these lakes by flowing out of the canyons, melting and leaving a moraine to form a natural dam. The view from Taggart Lake with Grand Teton as a backdrop is another great candidate for a prize-winning postcard. Refer to the Valley Trail, Taggart Lake, and Bradley Lake trail descriptions for more information on this leg of your trip.

After Bradley Lake, you reach the junction with the trail to Garnet Canyon and Surprise and Amphitheater Lakes. Go right (north) and hike the last 1.7 miles to the Lupine Meadows Trailhead. Walk about a mile over to the South Jenny Lake area where you left your vehicle to take the boat ride 4 days earlier.

Camping: The South Fork Cascade Camping Zone has at least fifteen indicated campsites, but you can camp anywhere in the zone, all the way up to a great site at the junction with the Avalanche Divide Trail. Most indicated campsites are four-star or five-star with nice views and privacy and good access to water, but shy away from any of the exposed sites if the weather looks ominous. To keep the distance fairly equitable each day of your trip, camp in the lower part of this camping zone.

Alaska Basin is outside of the park in the Jedediah Smith Wilderness, so you can set up a no-trace camp anywhere in the basin. If you camp at Sunset Lake, don't camp on the shoreline. There are several great campsites safely away from the beautiful but fragile alpine lake.

Phelps Lake has three excellent designated campsites—all of them are on the north shore of the lake with fire pits and room for two tents. Two share a food storage box; one has its own. The campsites are out of sight of the main trail, but they are fairly close, so please talk softly to respect the privacy of others.

There is no camping between Alaska Basin and Phelps Lake (11 miles) and between Phelps Lake and the Lupine Meadows Trailhead (10 miles). There is, however, one designated campsite at Bradley Lake, which the NPS reserves for hikers taking this or similar long backpacking trips through this section of the park. You can stay there and split the route from Phelps Lake to the trailhead into 2 days.

Options: I have never hiked up from Death Canyon to the Static Peak Divide, but while hiking down it I was left with the impression that I didn't want to do this trip in reverse, especially with a loaded backpack.

You have the option of shortening your trip by leaving vehicles at the Death Canyon or Taggart Lake Trailheads. You could lengthen your trip by 1 day by spending a night on the Death Canyon Shelf. If this interests you, keep going south from Basin Lakes until you find one of many five-star campsites on the shelf. Then, the next morning, go back to Alaska Basin and on to Buck Mountain Pass and the rest of the trip.

If the Phelps Lake campsites are taken, you can camp in the Death Canyon Camping Zone above the patrol cabin at the junction of the trail to Static Peak Divide. This adds 2 to 3 miles to the trip and would leave a very long last day if you go all the way to Lupine Meadows, but you can also spend a night at the Bradley Lake campsite reserved just for hikers doing long backpacking trips.

It's difficult to get the spacing correct on the last section of this trip, and it's easy to end up with more miles in 1 day than you really want. One option is to hang packs somewhere near the Death Canyon Trailhead and walk the rest of the trip with a daypack. If you do this, be sure to hang your packs out of reach of bears. Then, after reaching the Lupine Meadows Trailhead, drive back to the Death Canyon Trailhead for your overnight packs.

Side trips: Right after the boat ride, take the short side trip to Hidden Falls. You don't want to be the only people who haven't seen it. Also, you'll really miss something if you don't do the side trip up to Avalanche Divide, but it's a difficult climb to get there, making it an option for the fit and energetic only. If you have extra time after setting up camp in Alaska Basin, there are several short trails for other interesting side trips. In addition the basin is open, subalpine country, which makes off-trail hiking easy.

MILES AND DIRECTIONS

- **0.0** South Jenny Lake Visitor Center and Boat Dock.
- **0.1** Junction with Jenny Lake Trail; turn right.
- **0.6** Junction with Cascade Canyon Trail; turn left.
- **1.6** Junction with Inspiration Point Trail; turn right.
- **4.4** Junction with North Fork Cascade Canyon Trail; turn left.
- **7.9** Junction with spur trail to Avalanche Divide; turn right.
- **9.5** Hurricane Pass, Schoolroom Glacier, and the park boundary.

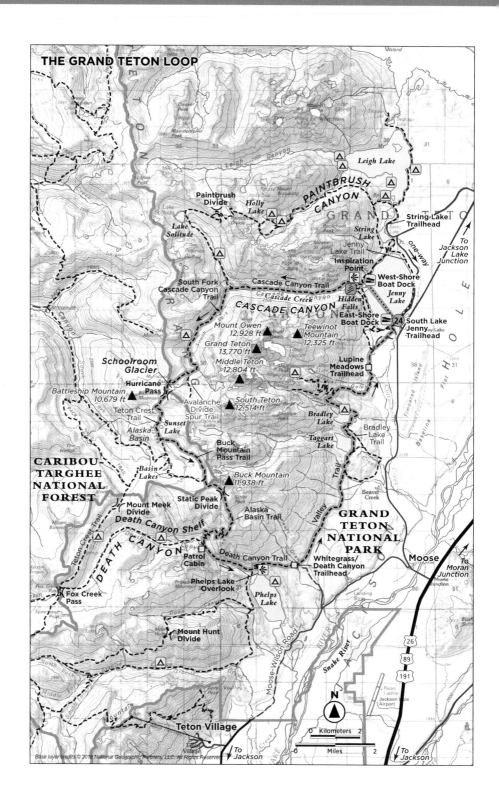

THE GRAND TETON LOOP

PAINTBRUSH CANYON

Leigh Lake

Paintbrush Divide

Holly Lake

String Lake Trailhead

Lake Solitude

String Lake

To Jackson Lake Junction

one-way

Jenny Lake Trail

Inspiration Point

South Fork Cascade Canyon Trail

Cascade Canyon Trail

West-Shore Boat Dock

Jenny Lake

Cascade Creek

Hidden Falls

CASCADE CANYON

East-Shore Boat Dock

Mount Owen 12,928 ft

Teewinot Mountain 12,325 ft

South Lake Jenny Trailhead

Grand Teton 13,770 ft

Schoolroom Glacier

Middle Teton 12,804 ft

Lupine Meadows Trailhead

Hurricane Pass

Battleship Mountain 10,679 ft

South Teton 12,514 ft

Teton Crest Trail

Avalanche Divide Spur Trail

Bradley Lake

Sunset Lake

Alaska Basin

Bradley Lake Trail

Buck Mountain Pass Trail

Taggart Lake

Basin Lakes

CARIBOU-TARGHEE NATIONAL FOREST

Buck Mountain 11,938 ft

Beaver Creek

Mount Meek Divide

Static Peak Divide

Alaska Basin Trail

GRAND TETON NATIONAL PARK

Death Canyon Shelf

Valley Trail

Moose

To Moran Junction

Teton Crest Trail

DEATH CANYON

Death Canyon Trail

Patrol Cabin

Whitegrass/ Death Canyon Trailhead

Fox Creek Pass

Phelps Lake Overlook

Phelps Lake

Moose-Wilson Road

Snake River

26

89
191

Mount Hunt Divide

Teton Village

N

Kilometers 2

Miles 2

To Jackson

To Jackson

Radio Facility

Jackson Hole Airport

Base layer credits © 2018 National Geographic Partners, LLC. All Rights Reserved.

South Fork of Cascade Creek
NATIONAL PARK SERVICE

11.2	Sunset Lake.
11.5	Junction with Buck Mountain Pass Trail; turn left.
13.3	Junction with Alaska Basin Trail; turn left.
13.9	Buck Mountain Pass and the park boundary.
14.7	Static Peak Divide.
18.7	Junction with Death Canyon Trail; turn left.
20.9	Junction with spur trail to Phelps Lake (trip to lake not included in mileage).
21.3	Phelps Lake Overlook.
22.5	Junction with trail to Death Canyon Trailhead; turn left.
26.2	Junction with Beaver Creek Trail; turn left.
27.0	Taggart Lake.
27.1	Junction with Taggart Lake Trail; turn left.
28.1	Bradley Lake.
28.2	Junction with Bradley Lake Trail; turn left.
29.5	Junction with Surprise Lake Trail; turn right.
31.2	Lupine Meadows Trailhead.
32.2	South Jenny Lake Trailhead, Visitor Center and Boat Dock.

COLTER BAY AND
JACKSON LAKE LODGE AREA

Heron Pond

25 LAKESHORE TRAIL

WHY GO?
A short, flat walk along the scenic shoreline of Colter Bay and Jackson Lake.

THE RUNDOWN
Start: Colter Bay Visitor Center
Distance: 2.0-mile figure-eight loop
Difficulty: Easy
Nat Geo TOPO! Map (USGS): Colter Bay

Nat Geo Trails Illustrated Map: Grand Teton National Park
Other maps: Earth Walk Press Grand Teton map; NPS handout map; Grand Teton Association's Colter Bay brochure

FINDING THE TRAILHEAD
Go 11 miles south of the park's northern boundary on US 89 or drive 5.2 miles north of the Jackson Lake Junction and turn west into the Colter Bay area.
After turning off the main highway, go 0.7 mile to the visitor center, taking the first right turn after passing by the general store. Park at the visitor center, which has restrooms. The general store is a short walk east of the visitor center. **GPS:** 43.899967 / -110.649783

THE HIKE
This hike is a great choice for an evening or early-morning stroll, especially for campers staying in the Colter Bay area or for families with kids. The kids can help fill up Jackson Lake by throwing countless stones into it.

The Lakeshore Trail actually starts out as a paved service road (no vehicles allowed) through the boat dock area and then turns into a well-used singletrack trail. About 0.1 mile after the road ends, you reach a trail sign and then a dike across a narrow section of land out onto a small island. The dike forms the center of this figure-eight route.

The trail circles the island (actually a small peninsula in Colter Bay), staying close to the water most of the way. Several beach areas invite you to stop and soak in the scenery of the Teton Range, especially Mount Moran, across the vast surface of Jackson Lake.

When you reach the dike again, turn left and finish the figure-eight route. You come

A kingfisher with a little snack
NATIONAL PARK SERVICE

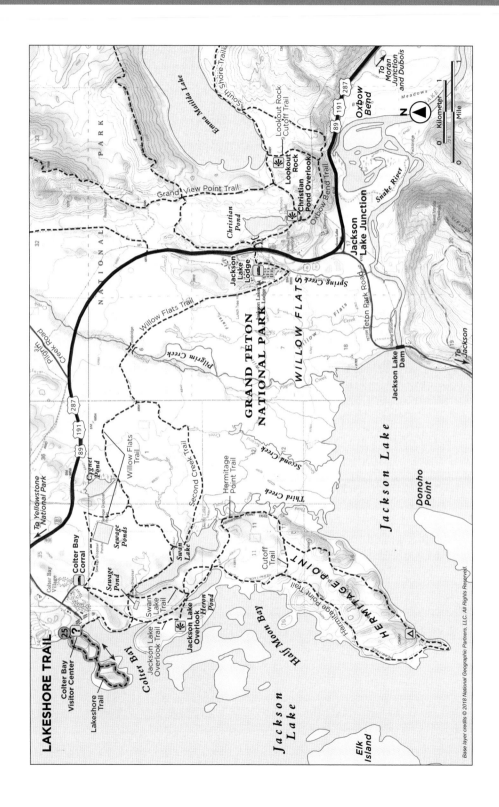

The Lakeshore Trail skirts the north edge of Colter Bay.

out by a NPS amphitheater where rangers give talks. Check at the visitor center for a schedule.

Camping: No camping allowed on this route.

Option: The figure-eight loop can be done in reverse with no increase in difficulty.

MILES AND DIRECTIONS

0.0   Colter Bay Visitor Center.

0.3   End of paved road.

0.4   Dike at center of figure-eight route.

1.5   Cross dike again; turn left.

1.9   Amphitheater.

2.0   Colter Bay Visitor Center.

26 LUNCH TREE HILL

WHY GO?
A short uphill walk into the park's history.

THE RUNDOWN

Start: Jackson Lake Lodge
Distance: 1.0-mile lollipop loop
Difficulty: Easy
Nat Geo TOPO! Map (USGS): Two Ocean Lake

Nat Geo Trails Illustrated Map: Grand Teton National Park
Other maps: Earth Walk Press Grand Teton map; NPS handout map; Grand Teton Association's Colter Bay brochure

FINDING THE TRAILHEAD

Drive 15.2 miles south on US 89 from the park's northern boundary or 1 mile north of the Jackson Lake Junction with US 287 and turn west into the well-marked Jackson Lake Lodge area. The trail starts on the viewing deck behind the lodge. Park in the Jackson Lake Lodge parking lot to use the restrooms or enjoy the restaurants and gift shops in the lodge. **GPS:** 43.877902 / -110.578244

THE HIKE

This short hike starts right on the incredibly scenic deck of Jackson Lake Lodge, which overlooks the expansive lake by the same name, with Mount Moran as a backdrop. It's steep but only a half-mile uphill to the interpretive displays on top of the hill.

Lunch Tree Hill marks the spot where John D. Rockefeller met with National Park Service director Horace Albright in 1926 (for lunch, of course) and apparently worked out a plan to create Grand Teton National Park, which Congress did 3 years later, in 1929. Rockefeller frequently came back to this spot for "renewed inspiration," but you don't have to be famous to get inspired by the fantastic view on top of Lunch Tree Hill. Anybody can do that. In fact, it will be hard *not* to feel a little renewed.

There are several interpretive displays on the hill, such as those explaining how the lake got its name (from early explorer David E. Jackson) and how the Teton Range got its name, which is a little hard to visualize. The early French explorers thought the range looked like *les trois tétons*—French for "the three breasts." Looking at the view from here, you'd say it must have been a long time since they'd seen any. The truth is the mountains were named based on the view from the west side, which makes a little more sense.

Camping: No camping allowed on this route.

Option: If the hike isn't long enough, you can continue walking north on the ridge on an excellent social trail for about another mile, which would make this a 3-mile round-trip.

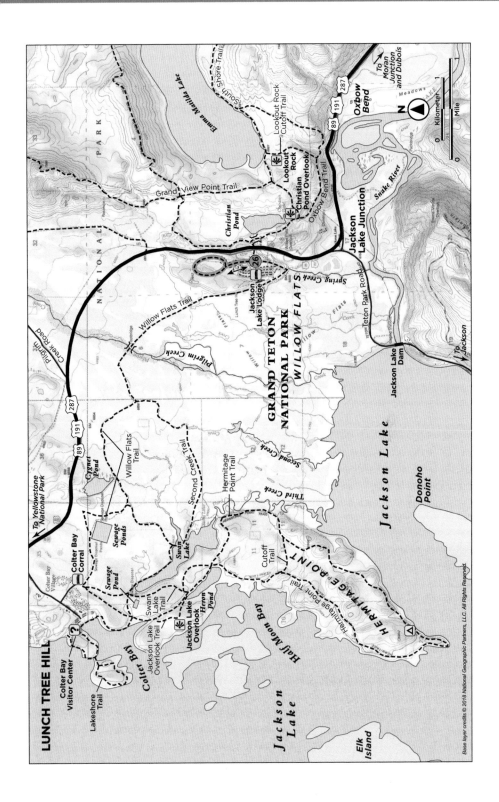

LUNCH TREE HILL

The massive high-altitude marsh out the back door of Jackson Lake Lodge
NATIONAL PARK SERVICE

MILES AND DIRECTIONS

0.0	Jackson Lake Lodge.
0.3	Start of interpretive loop.
0.5	Main interpretive display.
1.0	Jackson Lake Lodge.

27 CHRISTIAN POND

WHY GO?

A short stroll from Jackson Lake Lodge to a small lake for a good chance of seeing rare trumpeter swans; bring your binoculars.

THE RUNDOWN

Start: Jackson Lake Lodge corral
Distance: 1.2-mile out and back
Difficulty: Easy
Nat Geo TOPO! Map (USGS): Two Ocean Lake

Nat Geo Trails Illustrated Map: Grand Teton National Park
Other maps: Earth Walk Press Grand Teton map, NPS handout map; Grand Teton Association's Colter Bay brochure

FINDING THE TRAILHEAD

Take US 89 15.2 miles south of the north boundary of the park and turn right (west), or go 1 mile north of the Jackson Lake Junction and turn left (west) into the Jackson Lake Lodge. Follow the signs and park in the corral parking lot or in the main lot for the lodge. There are restaurants, gift shops, and restrooms in the lodge. **GPS:** 43.878065 / -110.573037

THE HIKE

Christian Pond is a small lake mostly covered with pond lilies and other vegetation. It often hosts nesting trumpeter swans that you can view from a safely distanced overlook.

To get there, take the very heavily used trail from the corral toward the highway underpass. Large trail-riding groups regularly leave from here, so plan on seeing lots of horses and being careful where you step. The trail immediately goes under the highway underpass, and just past it you reach a trail junction.

If you take the loop option (see below), you will return to this junction. Go right (southeast) here and hike another 0.4 mile through open country to the Christian Pond Overlook. Spend some time here reading the interpretive signs and studying the swans and other waterfowl commonly viewed on Christian Pond before retracing your steps back to Jackson Lake Lodge.

Camping: No camping allowed on this route.

Sky pilot
NATIONAL PARK
SERVICE

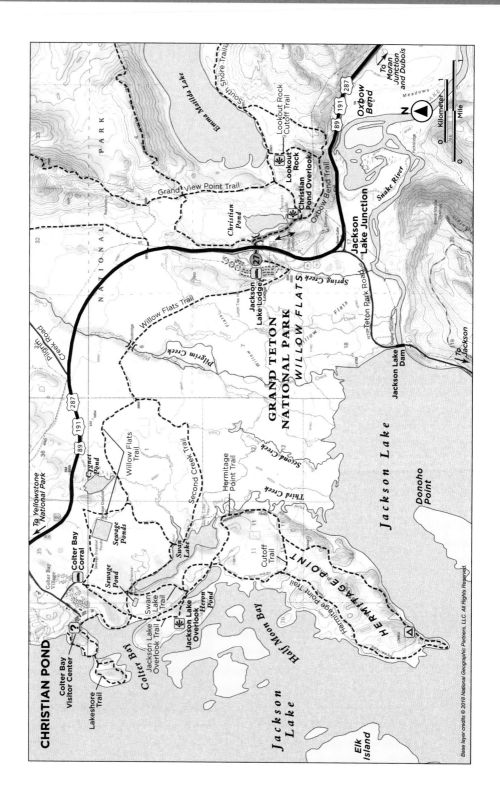

Option: If 1.2 miles aren't enough hiking for you, this trip can be extended to 3.1 miles. Continue past Christian Pond, turn left (north) on the Grand View Point Trail, and take another left (west) 1.4 miles later. This takes you back to the junction just east of the highway overpass.

MILES AND DIRECTIONS

0.0   Jackson Lake Lodge corral.

0.1   Highway underpass.

0.2   Trail junction.

0.6   Christian Pond Outlook; turn around and retrace your route.

1.2   Jackson Lake Lodge corral.

28 SWAN LAKE AND HERON POND

WHY GO?
An easy circuit with special treats for wildlife watchers.

THE RUNDOWN

Start: Hermitage Point Trailhead
Distance: 3.0-mile lollipop loop
Difficulty: Easy
Nat Geo TOPO! Map (USGS): Colter Bay

Nat Geo Trails Illustrated Map: Grand Teton National Park
Other maps: Earth Walk Press Grand Teton map; NPS handout map; Grand Teton Association's Colter Bay brochure

FINDING THE TRAILHEAD

Take US 89 into the park and turn west into the Colter Bay area, which is 11 miles south of the park's northern boundary or 5.2 miles north of the Jackson Lake Junction. After turning into Colter Bay from the main highway, drive 0.9 mile on a paved road, then turn left (south) at the first turn after passing the general store. The trailhead is a little hard to find the first time you go into the Colter Bay area. It's located at the south end of the big parking lot near the boat launch. Be careful not to take the trail that heads off to the east behind the trailhead sign. Instead, walk to the end of the parking lot toward the boat launch where trailhead signs mark the beginning of the trail. Go to the visitor center (just north of the trailhead) for toilet facilities. **GPS:** 43.901205 / -110.641466

THE HIKE

Be sure to take a map and plan on closely noting the directional signs along the route. There are several junctions along this short loop, and if you're enjoying the scenery too thoroughly (which would be easy), you might get on the wrong trail.

The trail starts out as a service road (it has a locked gate and is only occasionally used by vehicles). Along this stretch of trail, you can enjoy outstanding views of Colter Bay, with Mount Moran providing a classic backdrop.

At the end of the dirt road, you reach the first junction, where the loop section of this trip begins. Go right (south), unless you decide to take the route in reverse. The trail turns into a well-used singletrack but is still in excellent shape.

This area is heavily used by the Colter Bay horse concessionaire, so expect to see a few horses along the way—and a few horse apples on the trail.

After 0.2 mile you reach a fork in the trail. If you don't mind a little hill, go right for a nice view from the Jackson Lake Overlook. Either trail takes you to Heron Pond about a half-mile later.

Colter Bay, along the
first leg of this trip

Heron Pond is mostly covered with pond lilies. You can usually see pelicans, Canada geese, and other waterfowl species on the pond. In the evening hours, you might see beavers dining on the pond lilies, and you might also see a moose in the willows that surround the pond.

At the south end of Heron Pond, you reach a four-way trail junction. Take the sharpest left turn and head up a small hill toward Swan Lake. Like Heron Pond, Swan Lake is covered with yellow pond lilies. The lake gets its name from two trumpeter swans that lived here in the 1980s. The rare swans never produced any young, but they fiercely defended their territory, chasing away other swans that might have successfully nested in this prime habitat.

After the lake you pass by abandoned sewage ponds and then come to a junction with a trail heading off to the right (north) to the Colter Bay corral. Go left (west) and 0.1 mile later rejoin the abandoned service road for the 0.4-mile walk back to the trailhead.

Camping: No camping allowed on this route.

Option: This loop can be taken in reverse with no increase in difficulty.

Side trip: If you want a longer hike, you can add to your day by hiking down to Hermitage Point.

MILES AND DIRECTIONS

0.0   Hermitage Point Trailhead.

0.4   Junction with Swan Lake Trail; turn right.

0.6   Junction with Jackson Lake Overlook Trail, alternate route; turn right.

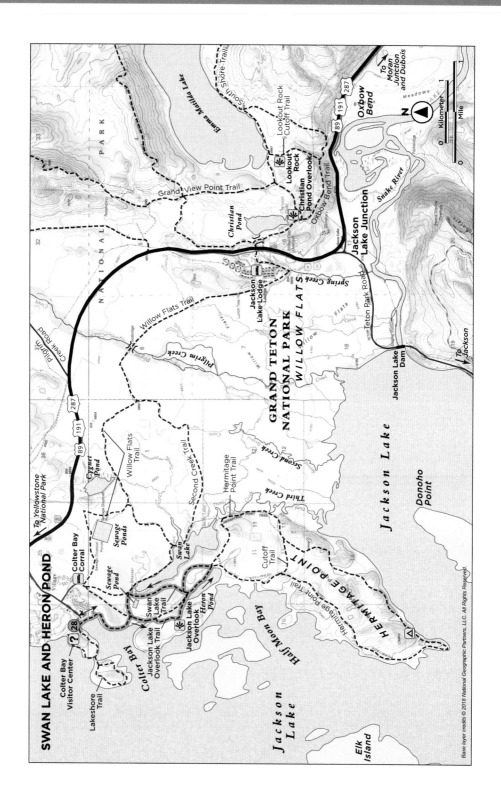

SWAN LAKE AND HERON POND

Enjoying the view over Heron Pond

0.9	Jackson Lake Overlook Trail rejoins main trail.
1.0	Heron Pond.
1.4	Four-way junction; turn sharp left.
1.9	Swan Lake.
2.5	Junction with trail to corrals; turn left.
2.6	Rejoin main trail to Colter Bay area; turn right.
3.0	Hermitage Point Trailhead.

29 WILLOW FLATS

WHY GO?
An easy walk through a wildlife-rich flatland.

THE RUNDOWN

Start: Jackson Lake Lodge
Distance: 4.9-mile shuttle
Difficulty: Moderate
Nat Geo TOPO! Map (USGS): Two Ocean Lake

Nat Geo Trails Illustrated Map: Grand Teton National Park
Other maps: Earth Walk Press Grand Teton map; NPS handout map; Grand Teton Association's Colter Bay brochure

FINDING THE TRAILHEAD

Drive 15.2 miles south on US 89 from the park's northern boundary or 1 mile north of the Jackson Lake Junction with US 287 and turn west into the well-marked Jackson Lake Lodge area. The trail actually starts in a small parking area on the south side of the main lodge. Leave a vehicle or arrange to be picked up at the Colter Bay corral. Colter Bay is 4.2 miles northwest of Jackson Lake Lodge on US 89. After turning west into the Colter Bay area, follow the signs and park in the corral parking lot. Park in the Jackson Lake Lodge parking lot to use the restrooms or enjoy the restaurants and gift shops in the lodge. **GPS:** 43.876833 / -110.577601

THE HIKE

The NPS usually closes this route for wildlife resource reasons until at least July 1, but the closure can last longer, so be sure to check on the current status before planning to take this hike.

This is a great hike for people staying at Jackson Lake Lodge or Colter Bay, but pick a cool day because the route goes through open meadows and willow flats with little shade along the way. Unlike trails in the high canyons of the Teton Range, snow leaves this area earlier in the spring and usually doesn't come as soon in the fall, which makes

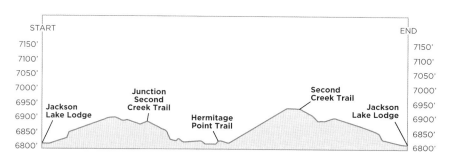

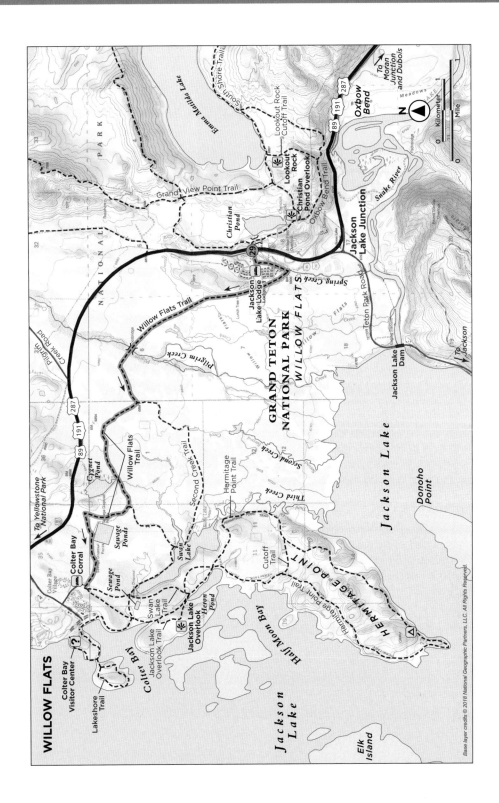

Colter Bay
Visitor Center

Lakeshore
Trail

Colter Bay
Village

Colter Bay

Colter Bay
Corral

Pilgrim Creek Road

To Yellowstone
National Park

287
191
89

Cygnet
Pond

Willow Flats
Trail

Sewage
Ponds

Sewage
Pond

Swan
Lake
Trail

Jackson Lake
Overlook Trail

Jackson Lake
Overlook

Swan
Lake

Second Creek Trail

Heron
Pond

Hermitage
Point Trail

Half Moon Bay

HERMITAGE POINT

Hermitage Point Trail

Cutoff
Trail

Third Creek

Second Creek

Jackson Lake

Donoho
Point

Elk
Island

Willow Flats Trail

Pilgrim Creek

Pilgrim Creek

29

Jackson
Lake
Lodge

GRAND TETON
NATIONAL PARK

WILLOW FLATS

Willow Flats

Willow Creek

Spring Creek

Teton Park Road

Jackson Lake
Dam

To
Jackson

Jackson
Lake Junction

Christian Pond

Grand View Point Trail

Emma Matilda Lake

South Shore Trail

Lookout Rock
Cutoff Trail

Lookout
Rock

Christian
Pond Overlook

Oxbow Bend Trail

Snake River

Oxbow
Bend

89 191 287

To
Moran
Junction
and Dubois

Meadows

N

NATIONAL PARK

Kilometer

Mile

Fall colors highlight Mount Moran as seen from the Jackson Lake Ledge area

this route ideal for spring or fall hiking.

As far as shuttle hikes go, this is one of the easiest. It's only a short drive from Jackson Lake Lodge to leave your vehicle at the Colter Bay corral. You can also leave the vehicle in the Colter Bay parking area, but that is about 0.4 mile farther.

The route starts right behind Jackson Lake Lodge on a mostly abandoned jeep road (now the Willow Flats Trail). This route is closed to vehicles with the exception of occasional use by concessionaires to serve meals to horse-riding groups. Actually, the entire route is on a dirt road, but it's still a pleasant hike, especially for hikers who get nervous about being too far from civilization and like perfectly flat hikes.

The first mile or so of the road goes through a large freshwater marsh. This is a wildlife-rich area, so you stand a good chance of seeing coyotes, moose, and other large wildlife species, as well as sandhill cranes and a wealth of small birds. You go by two classic beaver ponds and over Spring Creek on a bridge. You also get a great view of the Teton Range across Jackson Lake along the first part of the hike.

After crossing the freshwater marsh, you cross over Pilgrim Creek on a massive concrete bridge. Long ago this was the main route into Jackson Hole. After US 89 was constructed, this became a hiking trail with a monstrous, out-of-character bridge.

As you near the first junction, where the Willow Flats Trail meets the Second Creek Trail, you enter a mixed forest area dominated by a stand of stately cottonwoods. When you reach the junction, take a right (northwest) and head toward Colter Bay.

After the junction the cottonwoods gradually give way to conifers. At the second junction, where the Willow Flats Trail meets the Hermitage Point Trail, go right (north) and hike a little more than a mile to the corral.

Camping: No camping allowed on this route.

Option: You can start at Colter Bay instead of Jackson Lake Lodge with no increase in difficulty.

MILES AND DIRECTIONS

0.0   Jackson Lake Lodge.

2.4   Junction with Second Creek Trail; turn right.

3.7   Junction with Hermitage Point Trail; turn right.

4.9   Colter Bay Corral.

30 LOOKOUT ROCK

WHY GO?
An ideal small loop hike from Jackson Lake Lodge.

THE RUNDOWN
Start: Jackson Lake Lodge corral
Distance: 3.8-mile lollipop loop
Difficulty: Moderate
Nat Geo TOPO! Map (USGS): Two Ocean Lake

Nat Geo Trails Illustrated Map: Grand Teton National Park
Other maps: Earth Walk Press Grand Teton map; NPS handout map; Grand Teton Association's Colter Bay brochure

FINDING THE TRAILHEAD

Take US 89 15.2 miles south of the north boundary of the park or 1 mile north of the Jackson Lake Junction and turn west into the Jackson Lake Lodge. Follow the signs and park at the corral parking lot or the main lot at the lodge. There are restaurants, gift shops, and restrooms in the lodge. **GPS:** 43.878065 / -110.573037

THE HIKE
If you're looking for a short walk after dinner or in the early morning during your stay at Jackson Lake Lodge, you couldn't do much better than this hike. You get a chance to see rare trumpeter swans nesting on Christian Pond, study the great Oxbow Bend of the Snake River, and enjoy a view of massive Emma Matilda Lake from Lookout Rock.

From the corral, take the very heavily used trail to the highway underpass. Large trail-riding groups regularly leave from here, so plan on seeing lots of horses and being careful where you step. Just past the underpass, go right (southeast) at a junction and hike another 0.4 mile through open country to the Christian Pond Overlook. Spend some time here reading the interpretive signs and studying the swans and other waterfowl

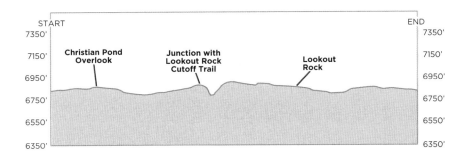

Arrowleaf balsamroot
NATIONAL PARK SERVICE

commonly viewed on Christian Pond, and then take the trail to the right (southeast) toward the Oxbow Bend of the Snake River.

This trail goes through the open sagebrush- and balsamroot-covered slope above US 287 and the Oxbow Bend of the Snake River. Take a few moments along the way to see how the Snake River has severely meandered and then cut through to create a small oxbow lake. You can often see pelicans and swans floating on the lake, even from a great distance. You also get a good view of Jackson Lake and Donoho Point Island, with the Teton Range as a dramatic backdrop.

After 0.9 mile you reach a junction with a trail to Lookout Rock. You can turn left here and cut about a quarter-mile off the trip, but I recommend continuing on the Oxbow Bend Trail. It's more scenic, with less horse use. These two trails join the South Shore Trail along the south shoreline of Emma Matilda Lake on each side of Lookout Rock.

Enjoy a rest and the vista from Lookout Rock Overlook before heading back toward Christian Pond. When you get to the Grand View Point Trail junction, go left (west)

LOOKOUT ROCK

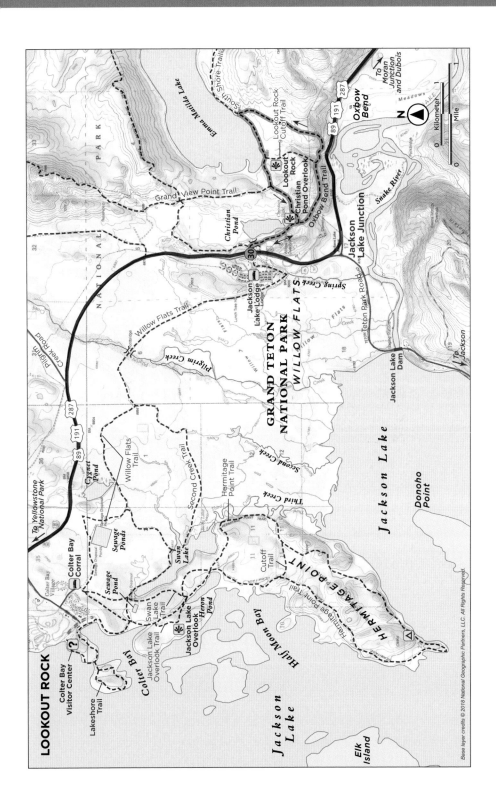

and hike another 0.6 mile back to Christian Pond. From here, retrace your steps back to Jackson Lake Lodge.

Camping: No camping allowed on this route.

Options: You can knock about a quarter-mile off the hike by taking the Lookout Rock Cutoff Trail; you can also do this loop in reverse with no increased difficulty.

MILES AND DIRECTIONS

0.0	Jackson Lake Lodge corral.
0.2	Junction just past highway underpass; turn right.
0.6	Christian Pond Overlook and junction with Oxbow Bend Trail; turn right.
1.5	Junction with Lookout Rock Cutoff Trail; turn right.
2.3	Junction with trail along south shore of Emma Matilda Lake; turn left.
2.4	Junction with Lookout Rock Cutoff Trail; turn right.
2.6	Junction with Grand View Point Trail; turn left.
3.2	Christian Pond Overlook.
3.6	Junction with trail before underpass.
3.8	Jackson Lake Lodge corral.

31 HERMITAGE POINT

WHY GO?

A unique hike on an undeveloped peninsula in expansive Jackson Lake.

THE RUNDOWN

Start: Hermitage Point Trailhead
Distance: 9.4-mile lollipop loop
Difficulty: Moderate
Nat Geo TOPO! Map (USGS): Colter Bay

Nat Geo Trails Illustrated Map: Grand Teton National Park
Other maps: Earth Walk Press Grand Teton map; NPS handout map; Grand Teton Association's Colter Bay brochure

FINDING THE TRAILHEAD

Take US 89 into the park and turn west into the Colter Bay area, which is 11 miles south of the park's northern boundary or 5.2 miles north of the Jackson Lake Junction with US 287. After turning into Colter Bay from the main highway, drive 0.9 mile on a paved road, then turn left (south) at the first turn after passing the general store. The trailhead is a little hard to find the first time you go into the Colter Bay area. It's located at the southern end of the big parking lot near the boat launch. Park here, along with the boaters. Be careful not to take the trail heading off to the east behind the trailhead sign. Instead, walk to the end of the parking lot toward the boat launch where you see the trailhead signs marking the beginning of the trail. Go to the visitor center (just north of the trailhead) for restrooms. **GPS:** 43.901205 / -110.641466

THE HIKE

The Hermitage Point area is a confusing labyrinth of trails. After hiking all of them, I recommend this route as among the best hikes in the park. This is essentially an extended version of Swan Lake and Heron Pond.

Be sure to take a map and closely watch the directional signs along the route. There are lots of junctions along this short loop, and if you're enjoying the scenery too thoroughly (which would be easy), you might get on the wrong trail.

The trail starts out as a service road (it has a locked gate and is only occasionally used by official vehicles). Along this stretch of trail, you can enjoy outstanding views of Colter Bay, with Mount Moran providing a classic backdrop.

At the end of the dirt road, you reach the first junction with the Swan Lake Trail, where the loop section of this trip begins. Go right (south), unless you decide to take the route in reverse. The trail turns into singletrack, but it's still in excellent shape.

About a quarter-mile later, you reach a fork in the trail. If you don't mind a little hill, go right on the alternate Jackson Lake Overlook Trail for a nice view from the Jackson Lake Overlook. Either trail takes you to Heron Pond about a half-mile later.

Heron Pond is mostly covered with pond lilies. You can usually see pelicans, Canada geese, and other waterfowl species on the pond. In the evening hours, you might see beavers dining on the pond lilies, or you might see a moose in the willows that surround the pond.

At the south end of Heron Pond, you reach a four-way trail junction. Take the extreme right turn, onto the Hermitage Point Trail, and keep heading south along the lakeshore. You return to this junction later in the hike. In 0.8 mile, turn right (south) again at the junction with the cutoff trail.

After leaving Heron Pond, the trail stays out of sight of Jackson Lake for a while and then enters open sagebrush country with stunning views of the Teton Range, especially Mount Moran, across Hermitage Point. It stays this way for about a mile to the point.

After a rest to soak in the scenery from the point, continue through the sagebrush meadows as you head back along the east side of the peninsula, past the designated campsite 9, to the junction with the cutoff trail. Go right (north) at this junction and hike another 0.7 mile to the second cutoff trail. Here, take a left (west) and go over a small hill and down to the four-way junction at the south end of Heron Pond. At this junction, take the first right (not the trail along the shore of Heron Pond) and go north back over the small ridge down to Swan Lake.

Heron Pond, along the
Hermitage Point Trail

Like Heron Pond, Swan Lake is mostly covered with yellow pond lilies. The lake gets its name from the two trumpeter swans that lived here in the 1980s. The rare swans never produced any young, but they fiercely defended their territory, chasing away other swans that might have successfully nested in this prime habitat.

After the lake you pass by abandoned sewage ponds and then arrive at a junction with a trail heading off to the right (north) to the Colter Bay corral. Go left (west) and 0.1 mile later rejoin the abandoned service road for the 0.4-mile walk back to the trailhead.

Camping: You can camp on Hermitage Point at campsite 9—definitely a five-star campsite (at least!) with a terrific view from a fantastic food area near the lakeshore. There is room for three or four tents and easy access to water. Campfires are allowed in the designated fire pit, and the site has two bear boxes for safe storage of food and garbage. Campsite 9 GPS: 43.857184 / -110.641743

Options: The Hermitage Point area is a labyrinth of trails with many options to shorten or lengthen your hike. Keep the map out and take your pick.

MILES AND DIRECTIONS

0.0   Hermitage Point Trailhead.

0.4   Junction with Swan Lake Trail; turn right.

0.6   Junction with Jackson Lake Overlook Trail, alternate route; turn right.

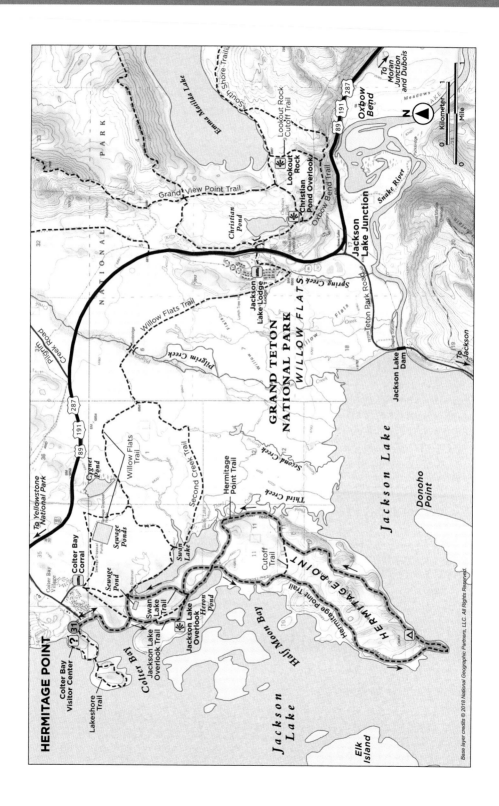

1.4	Heron Pond and a four-way junction; turn far right.
2.2	Junction with cutoff trail; turn right onto Hermitage Point Trail.
4.4	Hermitage Point.
4.9	Designated campsite 9.
6.6	Junction with cutoff trail; turn right.
7.3	Junction with trail to Heron Pond; turn left.
7.8	Heron Pond and four-way junction; turn first right.
8.3	Swan Lake.
9.0	Rejoin main trail to Colter Bay area; turn right.
9.4	Hermitage Point Trailhead.

32 GRAND VIEW POINT

WHY GO?
A short, steep hike with a view to dream for.

THE RUNDOWN

Start: Grand View Point Trailhead
Distance: 2.2-mile out and back with loop option
Difficulty: Easy
Nat Geo TOPO! Map (USGS): Two Ocean Lake

Nat Geo Trails Illustrated Map: Grand Teton National Park
Other maps: Earth Walk Press Grand Teton map; NPS handout map; Grand Teton Association's Colter Bay brochure

FINDING THE TRAILHEAD

Drive 0.9 mile north of the Jackson Lake Lodge turnoff on US 89 and turn right (east) on an unpaved road. When I hiked this trip, this turnoff was unmarked, but it's easy to find. It's the first right turn north of Jackson Lake Lodge. This is a rough jeep road, and a high-clearance vehicle is recommended. Drive 0.8 mile up this jeep road until it ends at the trailhead. If you have a high-clearance vehicle, park right at the trailhead. If not, park in one of the turnouts along the first part of the jeep road and walk up the road to the trailhead. There are no trailhead facilities. **GPS:** 43.898301 /-110.560961

THE HIKE

This is a wonderful short hike, but you have a serious hill to climb to earn the spectacular view from Grand View Point.

Just uphill from the trailhead (0.2 mile), you come to a junction with a trail heading south toward Emma Matilda Lake. Go left (north) here and start a gradual climb up to the top of Grand View Point. Just before you reach Grand View Point, you level off at a high point that could be confused with the real thing. Walk slightly farther down the trail for the real Grand View Point.

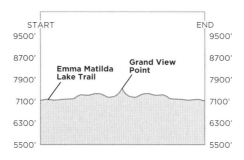

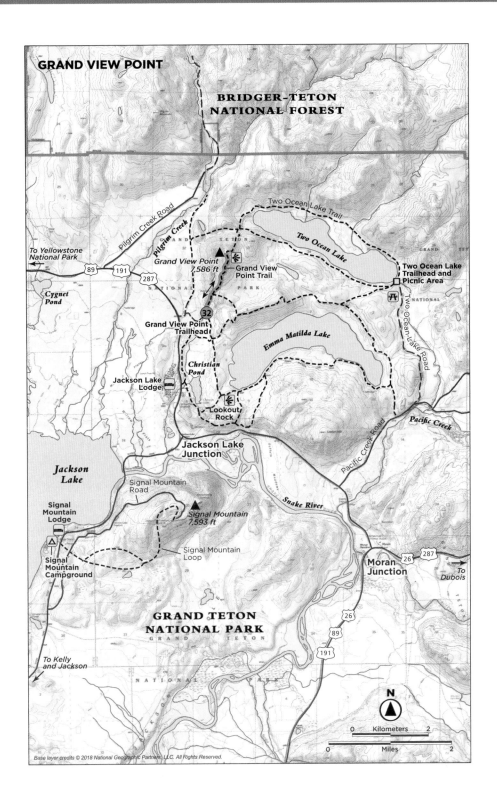

GRAND VIEW POINT

BRIDGER-TETON
NATIONAL FOREST

Pilgrim Creek Road

Pilgrim Creek

Two Ocean Lake Trail

Two Ocean Lake

Grand View Point
7,586 ft

Grand View
Point Trail

To Yellowstone
National Park

89   191

287

Cygnet
Pond

Two Ocean Lake
Trailhead and
Picnic Area

32

Grand View Point
Trailhead

Emma Matilda Lake

Christian
Pond

Jackson Lake
Lodge

Lookout
Rock

Jackson Lake
Junction

Jackson
Lake

Signal Mountain
Road

Pacific Creek

Pacific Creek Road

Signal Mountain
7,593 ft

Snake River

Signal
Mountain
Lodge

Signal Mountain
Loop

Signal
Mountain
Campground

Moran
Junction

26   287

To
Dubois

GRAND TETON
NATIONAL PARK

GRAND   TETON

26

89

191

To Kelly
and Jackson

NATIONAL   PARK

N

0   Kilometers   2

0   Miles   2

Morning clouds below world-renowned Grand Teton

From the top of 7,586-foot Grand View Point, you have the view you expect, an outstanding look at Mount Moran and the rest of the mighty Teton Range off to the west, although this is partially obscured by trees. However, to my surprise, you also get a terrific sweeping vista of Two Ocean Lake, the lush meadows surrounding this huge mountain lake, and the Teton Wilderness in the background.

After a short rest, enjoy the downhill walk back to the trailhead.

Camping: No camping allowed on this route.

Option: You can make a short loop out of this trip by continuing on the trail down the north side of Grand View Point for 0.9 mile to a junction with the Pilgrim Creek Trail. Go left (west) here and hike 1 mile until you get into a large meadow. Here the trail turns into an abandoned jeep road. Walk down the jeep road a few hundred yards until you see another road heading off to the south. Go left here, and in 0.8 mile you join the jeep road you drove up to the trailhead. Turn left (east) here and walk up the road to your vehicle. Distance of loop: 4.4 miles.

Side trip: You could hike down to the west end of Two Ocean Lake (2.6 miles round-trip from Grand View Point) before heading back to the trailhead.

MILES AND DIRECTIONS

0.0   Grand View Point Trailhead.

0.2   Junction with trail to Emma Matilda Lake; turn left.

1.1   Grand View Point; turn around and retrace your route.

2.2   Grand View Point Trailhead.

33 TWO OCEAN LAKE

WHY GO?

A medium-length hike around a large lake in a lesser-known section of the park.

THE RUNDOWN

Start: Two Ocean Lake Picnic Area and Trailhead

Distance: 6.4-mile loop

Difficulty: Moderate

Nat Geo TOPO! Map (USGS): Two Ocean Lake

Nat Geo Trails Illustrated Map: Grand Teton National Park

Other maps: Earth Walk Press Grand Teton map; NPS handout map

FINDING THE TRAILHEAD

From the Jackson Lake Junction, drive east on US 287 for 2.6 miles and turn left (north) on Pacific Creek Road. From the Moran Junction, drive west on US 287 for 1.2 miles and turn right (north) onto Pacific Creek Road. Once on Pacific Creek Road, drive 2 miles before turning left (north) on Two Ocean Lake Road, which ends at the picnic area and trailhead 2.4 miles later. Pacific Creek Road is paved, but Two Ocean Lake Road is not, but it is accessible by most vehicles when in good condition. In the spring, heavy rains sometimes turn this road into a quagmire and the NPS closes it, so be sure to check the status of the road at an entrance station or visitor center before making the trip. Park at the trailhead, which has picnic tables and a toilet. **GPS:** 43.901231 / -110.501607

THE HIKE

When I took this hike in late June, I didn't see another hiker, which is next to amazing considering how nice it is. The reason? When you think of hiking in Grand Teton, you don't think of gentle trails around forest-lined mountain lakes. Instead, you think of

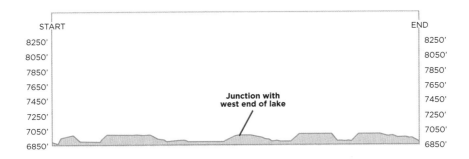

Hiking around Two Ocean Lake
NATIONAL PARK SERVICE

walking around the great peaks. Consequently, it appears that the northeast corner of the park has been spared the popularity of its western section.

You can take the loop in either direction. I liked the north shore better because it was more open and the Teton Range was visible across the lake on the horizon. Since the morning is clear more often than the afternoon, you might try the north shore first.

Along the north shore, the Two Ocean Lake Trail splits. Take the high route, as the low route is for horses and has no footbridges over streams and marshy areas. Most of the north-shore trail goes through meadows with consistently great scenery. The north-shore route is also slightly longer than the south shore. The south shore is more forested and has fewer views of the lake, but it has a few large meadows.

Watch for waterfowl on the lake and moose in the thickets lining both shores. Also, and most important, bring bear pepper spray and stay alert for signs of the great bear, as grizzlies are more common in this area than in other parts of the park.

Camping: No camping allowed along this route.

Options: You can take this loop in reverse with no extra difficulty. You can also start this loop at the Grand View Point Trailhead, a good option in the spring if the Two Ocean Lake Road is closed.

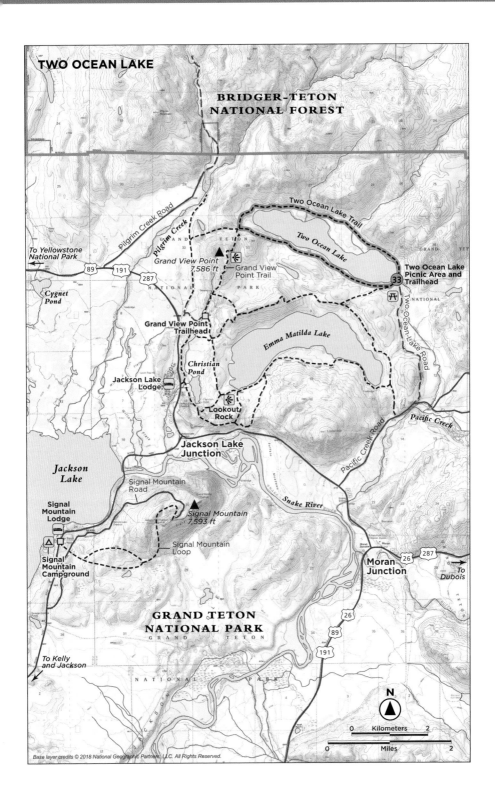

TWO OCEAN LAKE

BRIDGER–TETON
NATIONAL FOREST

Pilgrim Creek Road

Pilgrim Creek

Two Ocean Lake Trail

Two Ocean Lake

To Yellowstone
National Park

89
191
287

Grand View Point
7,586 ft

Grand View
Point Trail

Two Ocean Lake
Picnic Area and
Trailhead

33

Two Ocean Lake Road

Cygnet
Pond

Grand View Point
Trailhead

Emma Matilda Lake

Christian
Pond

Jackson Lake
Lodge

Lookout
Rock

Pacific Creek

Jackson Lake
Junction

Jackson
Lake

Signal Mountain
Road

Snake River

Pacific Creek Road

Signal
Mountain
Lodge

Signal Mountain
7,593 ft

Signal Mountain
Loop

Moran
Junction

26
287

To
Dubois

Signal
Mountain
Campground

GRAND TETON
NATIONAL PARK

26

To Kelly
and Jackson

89
191

N

0   Kilometers   2

0   Miles   2

Base layer credits © 2018 National Geographic Partners, LLC. All Rights Reserved.

Serviceberry
NATIONAL PARK SERVICE

Side trips: When you get to the west end of the lake, you can take a short side trip to the top of GrandView Point for a truly grand view of the lake you're hiking around. You can also take a 2-mile (round-trip) trail from the picnic area to see Emma Matilda Lake.

MILES AND DIRECTIONS

0.0 Two Ocean Lake Picnic Area and Trailhead.

3.3 Junction at the west end of lake; turn left.

6.4 Two Ocean Lake Picnic Area and Trailhead.

34 SIGNAL MOUNTAIN

WHY GO?

The only trail in this section of the park with a unique view of Jackson Hole.

THE RUNDOWN

Start: Signal Mountain Lodge
Distance: 7.4-mile double-lollipop loop
Difficulty: Moderate
Nat Geo TOPO! Map (USGS): Moran, WY

Nat Geo Trails Illustrated Map: Grand Teton National Park
Other maps: Earth Walk Press Grand Teton map; NPS handout map

FINDING THE TRAILHEAD

Take US 89 north of Jackson for 11.5 miles and turn left (west) at the Moose Junction. Drive past the Moose Visitor Center and through the entrance station (about a mile after turning off the highway). Follow this paved park road for another 17 miles from the entrance station and turn left (west) into the Signal Mountain Lodge area. If you're coming from the north, drive 2.6 miles from the Jackson Lake Junction and turn right (west) at the Signal Mountain Lodge area.

This trailhead is difficult to find. Actually, it's at a small sign on the east side of the road about 0.1 mile south of the Signal Mountain Lodge turnoff. There is no place to pull off or park a car right at the trailhead, so it's easy to miss it. You can also start this hike from the boat launch area, but again, no parking spots. The closest place to park is in the large lot in the lodge area. This adds about 0.4 mile to the distance of this trip. There are restrooms, a general store, a restaurant, gift shops, a gas station, and a ranger station in the Signal Mountain area. **GPS:** 43.840067 / -110.61595

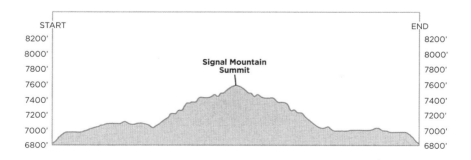

THE HIKE

This is the only official hike in this section of the park. From the top of Signal Mountain, you get a panoramic view of the entire valley—Jackson Lake and the Teton Range to the west, and the Oxbow Bend of the Snake River to the north. Yes, you can drive to the top of Signal Mountain on a paved road, but you miss out on a great hike and some exercise if you do.

From the lodge area, carefully walk across the highway to the trail. From here you climb gradually to the junction with the loop trail, which is 0.3 mile after crossing (again, carefully) paved Signal Mountain Road.

When you get to the start of the loop trail, you can take a left (northeast) on the ridge route or a right on the lake route. It makes no difference, but this trail description takes the clockwise route. This loop does not show on commercial maps for the area, but it is on the NPS handout map.

The ridge route goes through mature forest and large sagebrush meadows. When you get halfway around the loop, you see the spur trail going off to your left to the top of the mountain. You could skip the 1-mile extension up to the top of Signal Mountain, but you'd be missing the best part of the hike. The view from the top is so much more rewarding when you walk up there.

After you rejoin the loop trail, go left (south) and continue through a big meadow until you drop down to the more forested area around Keith Lake (watch for many species

Jackson Lake from Signal Mountain
NATIONAL PARK SERVICE

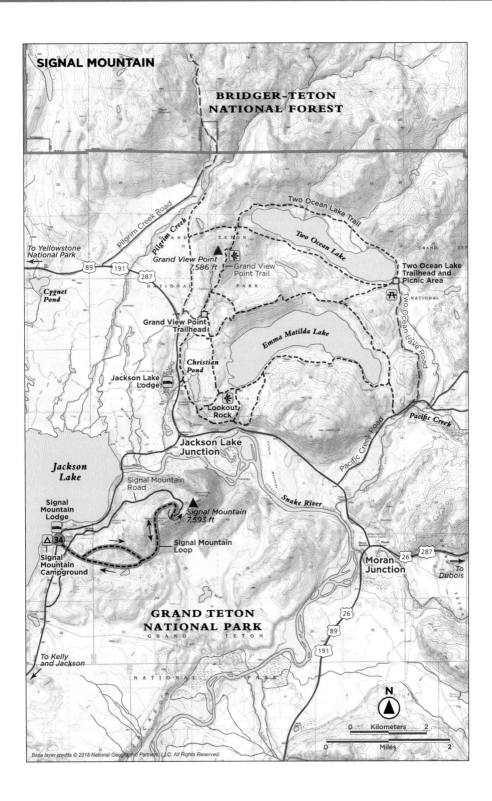

SIGNAL MOUNTAIN

BRIDGER-TETON
NATIONAL FOREST

Two Ocean Lake Trail

Pilgrim Creek Road

Pilgrim Creek

Two Ocean Lake

To Yellowstone
National Park

Grand View Point
7,586 ft

Grand View
Point Trail

Two Ocean Lake
Trailhead and
Picnic Area

Cygnet
Pond

Grand View Point
Trailhead

Emma Matilda Lake

Two Ocean Lake Road

Christian
Pond

Jackson Lake
Lodge

Lookout
Rock

Pacific Creek

Jackson Lake
Junction

Jackson
Lake

Signal Mountain
Road

Pacific Creek Road

Signal Mountain
Lodge

Signal Mountain
7,593 ft

Snake River

34

Signal Mountain
Loop

Moran
Junction

26   287

Signal
Mountain
Campground

To
Dubois

GRAND TETON
NATIONAL PARK

26

To Kelly
and Jackson

89

191

N

Base layer credits © 2018 National Geographic Partners, LLC. All Rights Reserved.

| 0 | Kilometers | 2 |
| 0 | Miles | 2 |

of waterfowl on the lake) and then back to the start of the loop. Go left (west) here and retrace your steps back to the lodge area. The trail is in great shape and easy to follow the entire way.

Commercial maps and the NPS handout show a trail going from the top of the ridge north to Oxbow Bend, but this trail has been abandoned because of the unsafe condition of the old bridge over the Snake River.

Camping: No camping allowed on this route.

Option: If you don't like hills, you can, of course, get a ride to the top and walk down to the lodge.

MILES AND DIRECTIONS (FROM SIGNAL MOUNTAIN LODGE)

0.0 Signal Mountain Lodge.

0.2 Trailhead on main park road.

0.4 Signal Mountain Road.

0.7 Start of loop trail; turn left.

3.2 Spur trail to top of Signal Mountain; turn left.

3.7 Summit of Signal Mountain; turn around and retrace your steps to the loop section of the route.

4.2 Loop trail; turn left.

6.7 End of loop; turn left.

7.0 Signal Mountain Road.

7.2 Trailhead on main park road.

7.4 Signal Mountain Lodge.

35 EMMA MATILDA LAKE

WHY GO?

Like the Two Ocean Lake hike, this route traverses the gentle, forested terrain around a large mountain lake on a little-used trail.

THE RUNDOWN

Start: Emma Matilda Trailhead
Distance: 10.5-mile loop
Difficulty: Moderate
Nat Geo TOPO! Map (USGS): Mount Moran; Two Ocean Lake
Nat Geo Trails Illustrated Map: Grand Teton National Park

Other maps: Earth Walk Press Grand Teton map; NPS handout map (some maps do not show the trail around the west end of the lake, so refer to the NPS handout map)

FINDING THE TRAILHEAD

From the Jackson Lake Junction, drive east on US 287 for 2.6 miles and turn left (north) on Pacific Creek Road. From the Moran Junction, drive west on US 287 for 1.2 miles and turn right (north) onto Pacific Creek Road. Once on Pacific Creek Road, drive 1.5 miles and park at a turnout on the left (west). When we checked the trailhead for this revision, there was no sign marking it. If you come to the Two Ocean Road turn, you've missed it, so backtrack 0.5 mile. Technically, the NPS doesn't consider this an official trailhead, which is why it and the first junction have no signs. Park at the trailhead, which has limited parking space. No trailhead facilities. **GPS:** 43.8701111, -110.5012222

THE HIKE

Emma Matilda and Two Ocean Lakes offer a gentle beauty quite unlike the high peaks for which Grand Teton National Park is so well known. Even though you definitely get the feeling of being in the backcountry, these trails aren't even shown on the NPS back-country brochure, which is maybe why I didn't see another hiker on the entire circuit around Emma Matilda Lake.

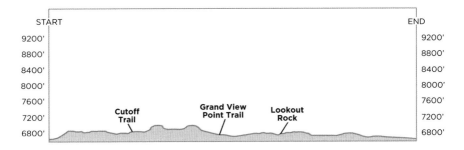

This hike, like Two Ocean Lake to the north, is in the northeast corner of the park, which has been spared the popularity of the hikes up the canyons of the Teton Range. I hiked the north shore first in the morning because it is more open and offers great views of the Teton Range across the lake.

From the trailhead, it's 0.5 mile to the junction with the loop trail around the lake. This junction is in a big meadow and was not signed when I was there. Several unofficial trails make it even more confusing, so be alert to get on the correct trail. To follow this hike description, go right (northwest) at this junction and start hiking along the north shore of the lake. Don't go extreme right and get on an unofficial trail, which takes you back to Pacific Creek Road. After the junction, you face a small climb to get to the ridge above the lake. At 2.2 miles, turn left at the cutoff trail to Two Ocean Lake.

Most of the north-shore trail goes through sagebrush meadows, aspen stands, and a mixed-conifer forest, often offering up a nice view of the lake with the Teton Range as the backdrop. The smell of sage accompanies you most of the way. In the fall, the aspens turn the landscape gold, and in the spring the abundance of arrowhead balsamroot gives a yellow flair to the entire north shore. One section of the north shore is well into the natural process of recovering from a forest fire.

When you get to the Grand View Point Trail, go left (south) on a trail (not shown on some maps) along the west end of the lake. In another 1.4 miles, you reach a confusing section of the trail. Stay alert between here and the Oxbow Bend Trail junction. This is

Emma Matilda Lake
NATIONAL PARK SERVICE

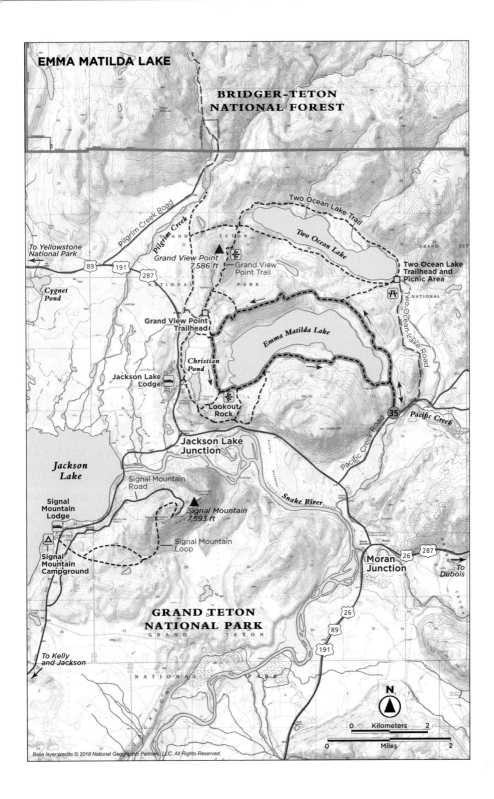

EMMA MATILDA LAKE

BRIDGER–TETON
NATIONAL FOREST

Two Ocean Lake Trail

Pilgrim Creek Road

Pilgrim Creek

To Yellowstone
National Park

89
191
287

Grand View Point
7,586 ft

Grand View
Point Trail

Two Ocean Lake

Two Ocean Lake
Trailhead and
Picnic Area

Cygnet
Pond

Grand View Point
Trailhead

Emma Matilda Lake

Christian
Pond

Jackson Lake
Lodge

Lookout
Rock

Two Ocean Lake Road

35

Pacific Creek

Jackson Lake
Junction

Pacific Creek Road

Jackson
Lake

Signal Mountain
Road

Snake River

Signal
Mountain
Lodge

Signal Mountain
7,593 ft

Signal Mountain
Loop

Moran
Junction

26
287

To
Dubois

Signal
Mountain
Campground

26

GRAND TETON
NATIONAL PARK

89
191

To Kelly
and Jackson

N

NATIONAL PARK

0   Kilometers   2
0   Miles   2

Base layer credits © 2018 National Geographic Partners, LLC. All Rights Reserved.

a triangular junction with the trail to Christian Pond and Jackson Lake Lodge. If you plan to take a short side trip to Christian Pond to see the swans or visit Jackson Lake Lodge before heading back to the trailhead, go right (west). If you aren't interested in a side trip, go left (east). In the next 0.3 mile, two more trails join the main trail from the south. Go left (east) at both the Christian Pond and Lookout Rock Trail junctions. In other words, to stay on the main route, take left turns only.

Lookout Rock lies between the two junctions and is a great place to relax and have lunch. You get a better view of the lake from this overlook than from anywhere else on the forest-lined south-shore trail until you get near the east end of the lake when the forest opens up to reveal the big jewel of a lake called Emma Matilda. Unlike the openness of the north-shore trail, the mature forest of the south shore blocks the view of the lake, but this is still a great walk in the woods.

Just before you get to the junction where you started the loop, you cross a footbridge over the outlet of the lake. When I hiked this trail, the local beaver population had appropriated the bridge as a good base for a dam. Unfortunately, the dam was backing up the entire lake, so the trail crew had to go in later that summer and undo these ultra-ambitious beavers' dreams. From this junction, take a right (southeast) and walk the last 0.5 mile to the trailhead.

Camping: No camping allowed along this route.

Options: You can take this loop in either direction with no extra difficulty. You can also hike the loop around Emma Matilda Lake by starting at the Two Ocean Lake, Grand View Point, or Christian Pond Trailheads. For an unusual option, hike half the loop, go over to Jackson Lake Lodge for lunch, and hike back to the east end of the lake.

Side trips: When you get to the west end of the lake, you can take a 3.6-mile trail (round-trip) to the top of Grand View Point for a great view of the Teton Range and Two Ocean Lake. You can also take a 2-mile (round-trip) trail over to see Two Ocean Lake. Lastly, you can take the short side trip over to see nesting trumpeter swans at Christian Pond.

MILES AND DIRECTIONS

0.0	Emma Matilda Lake Trailhead.
0.5	Beginning of loop around Emma Matilda Lake.
2.2	Cutoff trail to Two Ocean Lake Picnic Area; turn left.
4.9	Junction with Grand View Point Trail; turn left.
6.3	Junction with Christian Pond Trail; turn left.
6.5	Junction with Lookout Rock Trail; turn left.
6.6	Lookout Rock.
6.7	Junction with Oxbow Bend Trail; turn left.
10.0	End of loop around Emma Matilda Lake.
10.5	Emma Matilda Lake Trailhead.

Lewis monkeyflower
NATIONAL PARK SERVICE

36 **GLADE CREEK**

WHY GO?
A short, moderate hike in the northernmost section of the park.

THE RUNDOWN

Start: Glade Creek Trailhead
Distance: 7.0-mile out and back
Difficulty: Moderate
Nat Geo TOPO! Map (USGS): Flagg Ranch

Nat Geo Trails Illustrated Map: Grand Teton National Park
Other maps: Earth Walk Press Grand Teton map; NPS handout map

FINDING THE TRAILHEAD

From US 89, drive 4.4 miles west of Flagg Ranch on Grassy Lake Road (also known as Ashton-Flagg Ranch Road) and park at the trailhead on the left (south) side of the road. **GPS:** 44.089717 / -110.724238

THE HIKE

Most people don't think about this section of Grand Teton National Park, so plan on having Glade Creek and most of the North Trails section mainly to yourself.

This hike actually starts outside of the park in the John D. Rockefeller Jr. Memorial Parkway, a 24,000-acre slice of wilderness sandwiched between Grand Teton and Yellowstone National Parks. It's just as undeveloped as the parks—in fact, it is more wild than some parts of the parks. The trailhead sign says that it's 3.5 miles to the park boundary, but it seems shorter.

The trail starts out through a mature lodgepole forest, much of it burned by a forest fire. After about 1.5 miles, you cross Glade Creek on a footbridge. Shortly thereafter you drop down a fairly steep hill to a huge meadow. To the left you can see the Snake River flowing into Jackson Lake and a huge freshwater marsh, one of two large freshwater marshes found in the park. (The other is just south and west of the Jackson Lake Lodge.) You can also see Jackson Lake off to the south.

This is a wildlife-rich area, so take your time before retracing your steps to the trailhead. You may be able to see moose, swans, and other wildlife, especially in the early morning or near sunset. Even the mighty grizzly bear frequently roams through this rich habitat. But be forewarned: Another wildlife species frequents the area en masse—the mosquito. This is, in fact, the only section of trail in the park we had to get out mosquito repellent and netting.

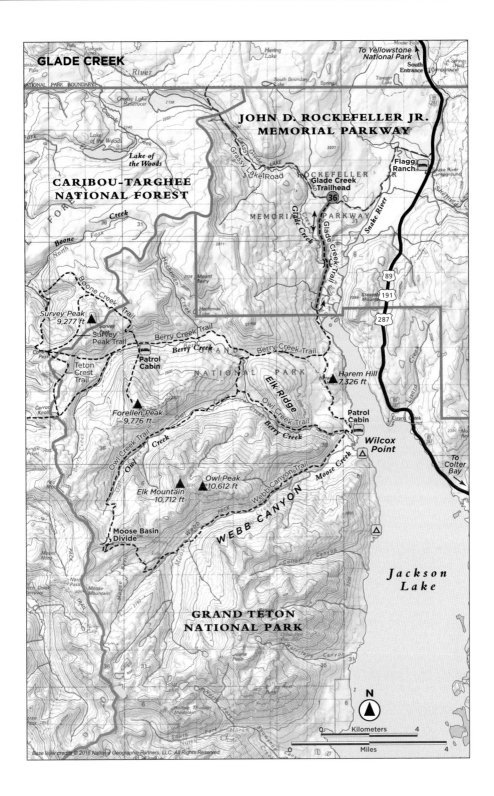

Trumpeter swans can be seen in this area of the park.
ISTOCK.COM/JACKVANDENHEUVEL

Camping: You may set up a no-trace camp anywhere along this route, before or after entering the park; you need a backcountry camping permit to camp in the park, but no permit is required for camping in the parkway.

Side trips: If you set up camp, you can hike up Berry Creek or take the Elk Ridge Loop hike before heading back to the trailhead.

MILES AND DIRECTIONS

0.0   Glade Creek Trailhead.

1.5   Cross the Glade Creek footbridge.

2.0   Break out into a big meadow.

3.5   Park boundary; turn around and retrace your route.

7.0   Glade Creek Trailhead.

37 **ELK RIDGE**

WHY GO?
A remote and seldom-hiked loop through the North Trails section of the park, a long day hike or overnighter.

THE RUNDOWN
Start: Glade Creek Trailhead
Distance: 19.3-mile lollipop loop
Difficulty: Difficult day hike; moderate overnighter
Nat Geo TOPO! Map (USGS): Flagg Ranch

Nat Geo Trails Illustrated Map: Grand Teton National Park
Other maps: Earth Walk Press Grand Teton map; NPS handout map

FINDING THE TRAILHEAD

From US 89, drive 4.4 miles west of Flagg Ranch on Grassy Lake Road (also known as Ashton-Flagg Ranch Road) and park at the trailhead on the left (south) side of the road. **GPS:** 44.089717 / -110.724238

THE HIKE
This trail loops around forested Elk Ridge in the remote North Trails section of Grand Teton National Park. It lacks the alpine vistas of many hikes such as nearby Moose Basin Divide and Jackass Pass, but it provides the quiet solitude of a walk in the woods with, most likely, only wild companions. You aren't likely to see many hikers on this route, but you might see Old Ephraim, the grizzly bear.

For details on the first section of this route, refer to the Glade Creek hike. About 0.5 mile after crossing into the park, the trail leaves the meadow and climbs up onto the slopes of Harem Hill through a short section of mature forest before emerging into another huge mountain meadow. The trail follows the east side of the meadow until you

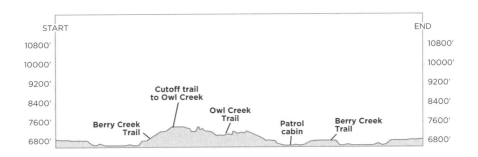

Lots of elk and not many
hikers on the Elk Ridge hike
ISTOCK.COM/DJ_38

see the junction with the Berry Creek Trail. Some older maps may show a triangle junction at this point, but the NPS removed this in 1995.

When you reach the Berry Creek Trail junction, go right (west) and continue hiking through a series of big meadows until you see a junction with the cutoff trail to Owl Creek. Go left (south) and cross Berry Creek (sorry, no footbridge), then climb a small ridge above the creek and back down into the confluence of Berry Creek and Owl Creek. At the junction, go left (east) and cross Berry Creek again just before it disappears into Owl Creek (sorry again, no footbridge).

If you're backpacking, the confluence area is a reasonably good point about halfway through this trip for your camp. You won't have trouble finding a great campsite in this area, which is at the east end of a huge meadow lining Owl Creek.

The trail gradually climbs up to a bench above Owl Creek and stays there until you drop down to a big, flat meadow on the shore of Jackson Lake. At the beginning of the meadow, go left (northeast) at the junction with the Webb Canyon Trail and left (north) again at the junction with the Glade Creek Trail at the patrol cabin.

It's about 2 scenic miles more (nice views of Jackson Lake) back to the junction with the Berry Creek Trail. Turn right (north) here and retrace your steps to Glade Creek and the trailhead.

Camping: You can set up a no-trace camp anywhere along this route, before or after entering the park.

Options: You can knock 9.8 miles off this trip by paddling a canoe from Leeks Marina on the east side of Jackson Lake over to Wilcox Point and doing only the 9.5-mile loop around Elk Ridge. This loop might be more difficult when done clockwise instead of counterclockwise as described here because of a fairly big hill coming from the south on the 2-mile cutoff trail between Owl Creek and Berry Creek. You can also make this a 3- or 4-day backpacking trip.

Side trips: If you're camping at Owl Creek, take a morning or evening stroll west on the trail along the stream and watch for wildlife.

An array of wildflowers along the trail

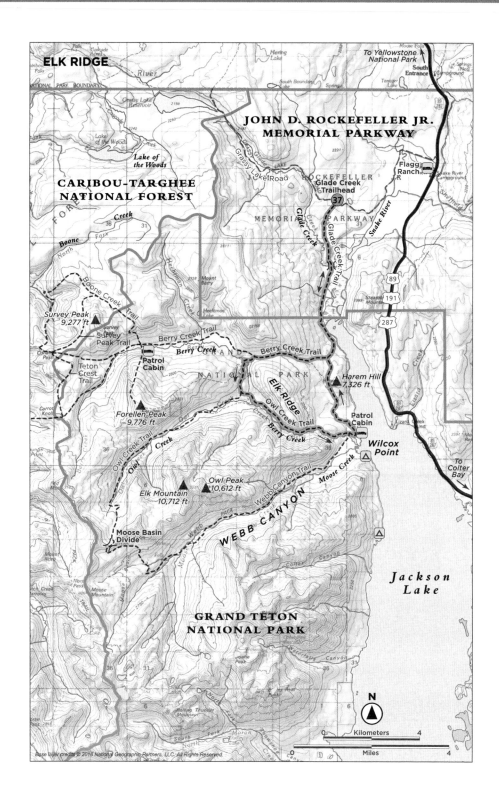

Uinta ground squir
NATIONAL PARK SERVIC

MILES AND DIRECTIONS

0.0   Glade Creek Trailhead.

1.5   Cross the Glade Creek footbridge.

2.0   Break out into a big meadow.

3.5   Park boundary.

4.9   Junction with Berry Creek Trail; turn right.

6.4   Junction with cutoff trail to Owl Creek; turn left.

8.4   Junction with Owl Creek Trail; turn left.

12.3   Junction with Webb Canyon Trail; turn left.

12.4   Patrol cabin and junction with Glade Creek Trail; turn left.

14.4   Junction with Berry Creek Trail; turn right.

15.8   Park boundary.

19.3   Glade Creek Trailhead.

38 JACKASS PASS

WHY GO?
A good choice for a long backpacking or base camp trip into the most remote and uncrowded section of Grand Teton National Park.

THE RUNDOWN
Start: Glade Creek Trailhead
Distance: 28.7-mile out and back with a small loop
Difficulty: Difficult
Nat Geo TOPO! Map (USGS): Flagg Ranch

Nat Geo Trails Illustrated Map: Grand Teton National Park
Other maps: Earth Walk Press Grand Teton map; NPS handout map

FINDING THE TRAILHEAD

From US 89, drive 4.4 miles west of Flagg Ranch on Grassy Lake Road (also known as Ashton-Flagg Ranch Road) and park at the trailhead on the left (south) side of the road. **GPS:** 44.089717 / -110.724238

RECOMMENDED ITINERARY
Set up a base camp in Lower Berry Creek and spend 2 or 3 nights there, exploring new sections of the park's north country each day, then retrace your steps out to the Glade Creek Trailhead.

THE HIKE
If you take this hike, prepare to savor the solitude of the wilderness. This route goes through the more gentle and uncrowded—but still exceptionally beautiful—North-Trails section of the park. I spent 4 days (including an August weekend) hiking the north trails and only saw one other group of hikers.

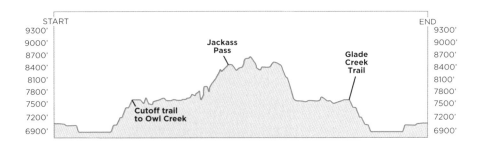

Hiking the North Trails area is one of your best chances to see the great bear in Grand Teton National Park.
ISTOCK.COM/NREFLECT

This hike actually starts outside of the park in the John D. Rockefeller Jr. Memorial Parkway, a 24,000-acre slice of wilderness sandwiched between Grand Teton and Yellowstone National Parks. It's just as undeveloped as the parks—in fact, it is more wild than some parts of the parks. The trailhead sign says that it's 3.5 miles to the park boundary, but it seems shorter.

The trail starts out through a lodgepole forest, a lot of it burned by past forest fires. After 1.5 miles, you cross Glade Creek on a footbridge. Shortly thereafter, you drop down a fairly steep hill into a massive meadow. To the left you can see the Snake River as it flows into Jackson Lake and one of two large freshwater marshes found in the park. (The other is just south and west of Jackson Lake Lodge.) You can also see Jackson Lake off to the south, and you may be able to see moose, swans, and other wildlife, especially in the early morning or near sunset. Even the mighty grizzly bear frequently roams through this rich habitat. But be forewarned: There is one wildlife species you will see and not enjoy—the mosquito. This is, in fact, the only section of trail in the park where I had to resort to mosquito repellent and netting.

About a half-mile after crossing into the park, the trail leaves the meadow and climbs up onto the slopes of Harem Hill through a short section of mature forest before emerging into another huge mountain meadow. The trail follows the east side of the meadow until you see the junction with the Berry Creek Trail. Some older maps may show a triangle junction at this point, but the NPS removed this in 1995.

Go right (west) and continue through a series of big meadows until you reach the junction with the cutoff trail going south over to Owl Creek. Go right (west) again and continue up Berry Creek all the way to the base of Jackass Pass.

The trail up Berry Creek is one of the nicest in the park, at least one of the nicest not many hikers will ever see. An immense, lush meadow lines Berry Creek all the way to the pass while Forellen and Survey Peaks supply the scenic backdrop. Watch for moose, elk, black bear, and, of course, the griz.

When you get to the junction with the trail veering off to the right and heading for the north side of Survey Peak, go left (west). If you decide to take the loop at the end of this trail, you'll be coming down that trail later in the day.

Shortly after this junction, you pass a patrol cabin off to the left and a sign for the trail up Forellen Peak; turn right here. The Forellen Peak Trail receives low-priority maintenance, so it can be hard to find, especially in the lower, forested sections.

From the cabin, you start your steady climb up to the park boundary at 8,500-foot Jackass Pass. This isn't really a difficult hill, and switchbacks make the steepest sections easier. The way up offers terrific views back down Berry Creek toward Jackson Lake. Unlike most passes and divides, however, Jackass Pass itself offers little scenery for the weary hiker. As the trail levels out and nears the pass, it slips into a lodgepole forest.

After a rest on the pass (or just before the pass if you want scenery), you have to make the decision whether to backtrack or try the loop trail around Survey Peak. If you choose the latter, as I did, continue past the pass to a junction with the Teton Crest Trail about 0.1 mile from the pass. Go right (north) and hike along a flat bench with sweeping vistas of the Jedediah Smith Wilderness in the Targhee National Forest off to the west and Survey Peak to the east. This section of trail is outside the park, but it's as scenic as any trail in the park. The trail goes through an unusually huge, flat bench on the Teton Crest. The first part of this leg is forested, but about halfway to Boone Creek it opens up and stays that way. As you near Boone Creek and drop down a steep slope to the junction, the trail becomes a little vague in spots.

At the Boone Creek junction, go right (east) onto the Survey Peak Trail and hike through a treeless "high-country prairie" as you climb up to the north flank of Survey Peak. The first part of this trail up to the park boundary is easy to follow, probably kept distinct by horse parties and hunters. As you near the boundary, however, the trail becomes indistinct. Watch for cairns, and stay in the little valley, which heads up to 8,700-foot Survey Pass at the park boundary. This is great elk country, as witnessed by a huge wallow just inside the park.

The trail drops sharply down to Berry Creek. This section of trail isn't well maintained or defined. If you decide to camp down at Berry Creek, you won't have to lug your big pack around this loop, and especially down this deadly downhill. You'll also be glad you did the loop clockwise and avoided this extremely steep climb.

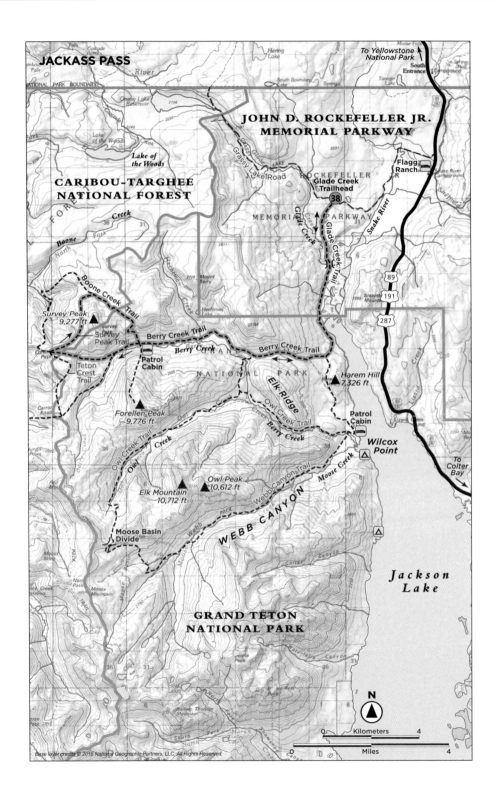

JOHN D. ROCKEFELLER JR.
MEMORIAL PARKWAY

CARIBOU-TARGHEE
NATIONAL FOREST

Flagg
Ranch

Glade Creek
Trailhead
38

Survey Peak
9,277 ft

Boone Creek Trail

Survey
Peak Trail

Berry Creek Trail

Berry Creek Trail

Patrol
Cabin

Teton
Crest
Trail

Harem Hill
7,326 ft

Elk Ridge

Owl Creek Trail

Forellen Peak
9,776 ft

Patrol
Cabin

Owl Creek Trail

Wilcox
Point

Webb Canyon Trail

Moose Creek

To
Colter
Bay

Owl Peak
10,612 ft

Elk Mountain
10,712 ft

WEBB CANYON

Moose Basin
Divide

Jackson
Lake

GRAND TETON
NATIONAL PARK

N

Kilometers   4

Miles   4

Base layer credits © 2018 National Geographic Partners, LLC. All Rights Reserved.

When you reach the Berry Creek Trail, go left (east) and retrace your steps back to the Glade Creek Trailhead. I noticed that the miles went by much faster than expected, and I theorized that the mileage might be slightly overstated on the trail signs. As you near the trailhead, you'll notice the hill climbing up to Glade Creek from the Snake River. It doesn't seem that big coming down, but at the end of a 3-day backpack, it seems much steeper.

Camping: This is an open camping area, so you may set up a no-trace camp anywhere along this route, before or after entering the park, but be sure to get a backcountry camping permit. It won't be difficult to find scenic campsites, especially at Berry Creek. If you decide to carry your overnight pack around Survey Peak, you can camp anywhere along the Teton Crest, but water can be scarce late in the season in this high country.

Option: Rather than carry your overnight pack to Jackass Pass, set up a base camp in Berry Creek and day hike the loop around Survey Peak.

Side trips: In addition to the loop around Survey Peak, you can hike south along the Teton Crest Trail from Jackass Pass, but this is an out-and-back side trip. If you set up a base camp in Berry Creek, you can hike up Berry Creek to Jackass Pass and Survey Peak, but you could take another day and go over to Owl Creek or hike the Elk Ridge Loop.

MILES AND DIRECTIONS

0.0	Glade Creek Trailhead.
1.5	Cross the Glade Creek footbridge.
2.0	Break out into a big meadow.
3.5	Park boundary.
4.9	Berry Creek Trail; turn right.
6.5	Junction with cutoff trail to Owl Creek; turn right.
11.1	Junction with Survey Peak Trail; turn left.
11.5	Patrol cabin and junction and trail to Forellen Peak; turn right.
13.1	Jackass Pass.
13.2	Junction with Teton Crest Trail; turn right.
15.4	Junction with Boone Creek Trail; turn right.
17.6	Junction with Berry Creek Trail; turn left.
22.2	Junction with cutoff trail to Owl Creek; turn left.
23.8	Junction with Glade Creek Trail; turn left.
25.2	Park boundary.
28.7	Glade Creek Trailhead.

39 MOOSE BASIN DIVIDE

WHY GO?

A long, hard backpacking adventure into the most remote section of Grand Teton National Park.

THE RUNDOWN

Start: Glade Creek Trailhead
Distance: 39.0-mile lollipop loop
Difficulty: Difficult
Nat Geo TOPO! Map (USGS): Flagg Ranch

Nat Geo Trails Illustrated Map: Grand Teton National Park
Other maps: Earth Walk Press Grand Teton map; NPS handout map

FINDING THE TRAILHEAD

From US 89, drive 4.4 miles west of Flagg Ranch on Grassy Lake Road (also known as Ashton-Flagg Ranch Road) and park at the trailhead on the left (south) side of the road. **GPS:** 44.089717 / -110.724238

RECOMMENDED ITINERARY: A 5-DAY TRIP AS FOLLOWS:

First night: Lower Moose Creek before entering Webb Canyon
Second night: Moose Basin
Third night: About halfway down Owl Creek
Fourth night: Jackson Lake shoreline north of patrol cabin

THE HIKE

If you're tired of the crowded trails around Jenny Lake or Jackson Lake Lodge, you'll really like this hike. In fact, you're likely to have the trail all to yourself. Like other hikes in the North Trails area, prepare to savor the solitude of the wilderness. This route goes through the more gentle and uncrowded—but still exceptionally beautiful—section of the park.

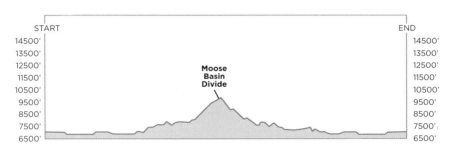

This hike actually starts outside of the park in the John D. Rockefeller Jr. Memorial Parkway, a 24,000-acre slice of wilderness sandwiched between Grand Teton and Yellowstone National Parks. It's just as undeveloped as the parks—in fact, it is more wild than some parts of the parks. The trailhead sign says that it's 3.5 miles to the park boundary, but it seems shorter.

The trail starts out through a lodgepole forest, a lot of it burned by past forest fires. After 1.5 miles, you cross Glade Creek on a footbridge. Shortly thereafter, you drop down a fairly steep hill into a massive meadow. To the left you can see the Snake River as it flows into Jackson Lake and one of two large freshwater marshes found in the park. (The other is just south and west of Jackson Lake Lodge.) You can also see Jackson Lake off to the south, and you may be able to see moose, swans, and other wildlife, especially in the early morning or near sunset. Even the mighty grizzly bear frequently roams through this rich habitat. But be forewarned: There is one wildlife species you will see and not enjoy—the mosquito. This is, in fact, the only section of trail in the park where I had to resort to mosquito repellent and netting.

About a half-mile after crossing into the park, the trail leaves the meadow and climbs up onto the slopes of Harem Hill through a short section of mature forest before emerging into another huge mountain meadow. The trail follows the east side of the meadow until you see the junction with the Berry Creek Trail. Some older maps may show a triangle junction at this point, but the NPS removed this in 1995.

At the junction with the Berry Creek Trail, go left (south) and continue to hike through a mature forest interspersed with huge meadows. The trail is in great shape all the way to the patrol cabin, and you get some nice views of Jackson Lake over the last mile or so before the cabin, making it seem like a short 7 miles from Glade Creek to the patrol cabin.

At the junction in front of the patrol cabin, go right (west) and hike another 0.1 mile to the junction with the loop trail over Moose Basin Divide. If you're following this clockwise route, go left (south) and ford Berry Creek. Sorry, no footbridge, so you get your feet wet just before setting up camp.

After Berry Creek, the trail goes through an open bench and then over into Moose Creek. This vicinity is a good choice for camping the first night out.

From here, you go about a mile up the trail before entering Webb Canyon, a steep and narrow section of the Moose Creek drainage, and stay there for several miles. The trail stays close to the stream most of the way, and Moose Creek is mighty impressive as it crescendos out of the high country. It's a constant cascade through the steep canyon—almost makes you forget the big hill you're climbing.

After about 6 or 7 miles of canyon hiking, you break out into gorgeous subalpine country in Moose Basin. You can camp anywhere in the basin, and it will definitely be a memorable night in paradise. When I was there, it was a monstrous "moose-less" meadow, but I'm betting that in many cases, you can see moose, elk, and other large wildlife in this rich high country—including the grizzly, so be alert.

From the basin, it's 2 to 3 miles to the divide. In the last 2 miles, the trail becomes a series of cairns in spots, and it's a wildflower carpet all the way. Actually, the hill isn't that

Moose and other wildlife abound along the Moose Basin Divide. ISTOCK.COM/ GARY GRAY

bad once you get to Moose Basin. Most of the serious climbing is behind you in Webb Canyon.

Save some water for lunch at the top. Late in the season, water is scarce for a mile or so on each side of the divide.

After a good rest on the 9,700-foot divide, drop down sharply toward upper Owl Creek and onto a bench covered with whitebark pine, a favorite food of Old Griz. Keep the bear pepper spray accessible and be especially alert late in the year when the bears are fattening up here on whitebark pine nuts for their winter sleep.

Owl Creek is the mirror image of Moose Creek. Instead of climbing steeply through a forested canyon and then mellowing out for a gentle push to the top, Owl Creek drops sharply at the top and then becomes a gentle open valley. Owl Creek is really a gigantic meadow with lots of great campsites and probably more moose than Moose Creek and more berries than Berry Creek. You have two stream crossings (one on Owl Creek and one on Berry Creek)—again, no footbridges.

When you reach the junction with the cutoff trail to Berry Creek, go right (east) and ford Berry Creek before it merges with Owl Creek. From this point, Berry Creek goes into a narrow canyon. The trail climbs way above the waterway and stays there for about 4 miles until it drops down to the junction with the Webb Canyon Trail. From here, retrace your steps back to the Glade Creek Trailhead.

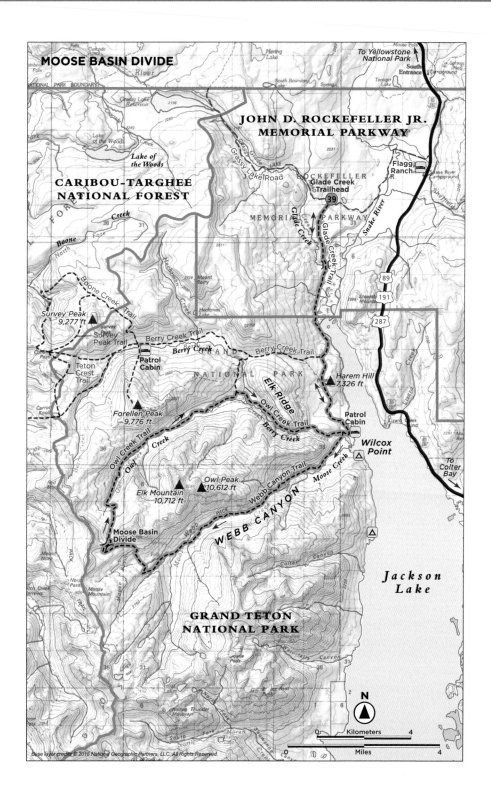

MOOSE BASIN DIVIDE

JOHN D. ROCKEFELLER JR.
MEMORIAL PARKWAY

CARIBOU-TARGHEE
NATIONAL FOREST

GRAND TETON
NATIONAL PARK

Jackson
Lake

Base layer credits © 2018 National Geographic Partners, LLC. All Rights Reserved.

Camping: This is an open camping area, so you may set up a no-trace camp anywhere along this route, before or after entering the park, but you need a permit after crossing the park boundary. It won't be difficult to find scenic campsites, especially at Owl Creek and upper Moose Creek. You can find a good camp in the low country around the patrol cabin or by going up the Webb Canyon Trail for less than 0.1 mile. Once in Webb Canyon, however, campsites are marginal. When you break out of the canyon, campsites are plentiful and very scenic. Likewise, when you drop down into Owl Creek, it's easy to find a five-star campsite, but campsites are scarce in the section between the cutoff trail to Berry Creek and the patrol cabin.

Options: You can cut 16 miles off your trip by getting a boat ride or taking a canoe across Jackson Lake from Leeks Marina to Wilcox Point. Be sure to go early in the morning and in good weather. You don't want to get caught in a storm canoeing across Jackson Lake. You can also take the loop in reverse, but I believe the hill is more precipitous on the Owl Creek side, and it's 14 miles uphill instead of 11 from the Owl Creek/Webb Canyon Trails junction. You can also go back via the Berry Creek cutoff trail instead of taking the last 4 miles down Berry Creek to the patrol cabin. This only adds about a mile to your trip, but it does mean a big climb to get over a ridge.

Side trips: There are several appealing off-trail side trips in the alpine country on both sides of Moose Basin Divide.

MILES AND DIRECTIONS

0.0	Glade Creek Trailhead.
1.5	Cross the Glade Creek footbridge.
2.0	Break out into a big meadow.
3.5	Park boundary.
4.9	Junction with Berry Creek Trail; turn left.
6.9	Jackson Lake, patrol cabin, and Owl Creek Trail junction; turn right.
7.0	Junction with Webb Canyon Trail; turn left and ford creek.
8.0	Webb Canyon.
18.0	Moose Basin Divide and Owl Creek Trail.
28.0	Cutoff trail to Berry Creek; turn right.
32.0	Junction with Webb Canyon Trail; turn left.
32.1	Jackson Lake and patrol cabin.
34.1	Junction with Berry Creek Trail; turn right.
35.5	Park boundary.
39.0	Glade Creek Trailhead.

PRESERVING GRAND TETON NATIONAL PARK

The Grand Teton Association is a nonprofit organization founded to assist with educational, historical, and scientific programs in and around Grand Teton National Park. The association operates bookstores in the park and in the nearby National Elk Refuge and Bridger-Teton National Forest. When you buy a book, video, or map from one of these bookstores, the profit goes to benefit educational and interpretive programs in the park. Your purchase also supports the publication of educational brochures available at information counters and entrance stations. You can obtain more information or a mail-order catalog of products offered by the association by writing Grand Teton Association, PO Box 170, Moose, WY 83012, calling (307) 739-3606, or going to www.grandtetonpark.org.

North Fork Cascade Canyon
NATIONAL PARK SERVICE

AFTERWORD

PLEASE LET IT BECOME A TREND

DON'T JUSTIFY

I've often said and long believed that we need to preserve all remaining wilderness because "they ain't making any more of it."

Well, after spending a wonderful day hiking the trails of the recently opened (2008) Laurance S. Rockefeller Preserve (LSR Preserve), I might have to rethink that philosophy. The late Mr. Rockefeller, his family, and the National Park Service seem to have just proved that you can create more wilderness.

Since being homesteaded by David W. Spalding in 1924, the LSR Preserve has been private land—first a homestead, then a guest ranch, then a private retreat for rich folks and their families and friends. Today it is new wilderness owned by all of us because one of the super rich wanted to give it back to nature and the American people.

And it was all done in such a grand way.

The area isn't huge in size (only 1,106 acres), but it is huge in significance. A very wealthy person bequeathed the land to Grand Teton National Park instead of including it in his estate to continue as a private getaway or selling it for many millions to a real estate developer or other extremely rich person who wanted a majestic hideaway on the slopes of America's most famous mountain skyline.

Now, officially part of Grand Teton National Park, the LSR Preserve and its small labyrinth of trails adds to the already amazing hiking opportunities in the park, and everything about it was done as carefully and naturally as possible.

Just chew on this for a few minutes: Thirty buildings plus several roads and utilities were actually removed and their imprints reclaimed. Then, the NPS planned and developed an excellent system of trails and facilities, all with the "let's do it as good as we can do it by nature" mission. The interpretive center, three high-tech, environmentally friendly toilets, viewpoints, walkways over bogs, and bridges not only make hiking easier for all hikers but also proficiently blend into the natural landscape. Even the trail signs are knee high to make them less obtrusive. The interpretive center, with its expertly thought-out displays, is the first platinum-level Leadership in Energy and Environmental Design (LEED)–certified building ever constructed in the NPS.

As I hiked all the trails and started writing up a couple of suggested routes for this book, I kept thinking about what had just happened. And then I kept asking myself, why can't Warren Buffett or Mark Zuckerberg or Oprah Winfrey or George Lucas or Larry Ellison or Bill Gates or Michael Bloomberg or Elon Musk or Paul Allen or Jeff Bezos

Mountain aster, one of the park's
most common flowers
CASEY SCHNEIDER

or Phil Knight or Charles Schwab or Mark Cuban or the Koch Brothers or the Walton Family or any other multi-billionaire out there wondering what to do with her or his money follow LSR's lead. Need a lasting legacy? Please peel off a billion or two and buy up some pricey real estate adjacent to a national park or wilderness area, then donate it to the public trust and help fund trails and facilities for the enjoyment of all.

On the remote chance one of these billionaires reads these few paragraphs, just think, being a billionaire isn't everything, but having a chunk of wild America bearing your name in perpetuity? That's really something. As the grandkids of the future hike through it, they'll ask their parents who was Jeff Bezos, Elon Musk or Mark Zuckerberg and why was this place named for him?

And the answer would be, they thought it was a better way to spend their billions than trying to colonize Mars. They thought it was more important to preserve this planet first.

So, on behalf of all hikers, today and in the future, and the millions who want and need more wilderness, thank you very much, Laurance S. Rockefeller and family. You proved it could be done. Now, we have to hope you started a trend.

—*Bill Schneider*

ACKNOWLEDGMENTS

Most guidebooks, including this one, result from a combination of effort, not the work of one person.

I would like to thank the National Park Service (NPS) for helping me research and review this book, especially Katy Duffy, Don Burgette, Mark Mangleson, Larry Castle-Ferricks, and Sara Petsch. Also, Sharlene Milligan and Jan Lynch from the Grand Teton Association were most helpful with their review and guidance.

I also extend my gratitude to the editors, cartographers, designers, and proofreaders at Falcon Publishing and Globe Pequot for putting up with a difficult author.

And, of course, what would I do without Marnie, Greg, and Heidi, my Schneider family hiking companions, who kept me company on many long days and big hills while hiking all the trails of Grand Teton? Thanks all.

HIKE INDEX